Bibli

The Satanic Book of the Way the Truth and Abundant Life

LCFNS
Lucifer Nostra Salus

„For the devil's word is alive and has sinful power, sharper than the nails of golgoth, it penetrates deep, separates flesh from spirit, bone from soul, recognises the instincts and intentions of the unconscious. There is no being hidden from its truth".

Etd 4.12

Contents

Preface 1

Genesis Secundum Serpentem .... Gss   6

Antichristus ....Ant   31

Epistle to the Undead ....Etd   60

Angelus Satanae-Encyclica ....Ase   69

Epistle to the Ungodly ....Etu   85

Pseudoapocalypsis .... Psa   90

Preface

Biblia Satanae. The Satanic Book of the Way, the Truth, and Abundant Life.

Biblia Satanae, not by an imaginary deity, but by Man, is inspired, useful for satanic teaching, for detecting theistic superstition, for educating in godlessness, for proclaiming the good news of Lightbearer who has revealed Himself to free from belief in an imaginary god, from fear of death and divine fire, from guilt for sin that never was, from belief in eternal life on one's knees. So that the Satanist would be perfect, for a life abundant in flesh and blood prepared.

The Bible of Abrahamic theistic superstition proclaims:

"And every spirit who does not recognise Jesus is not of God; and this is the spirit of Antichrist, who, as you have heard, is coming and is already in the world'. 1 John 4:3

"Who is a liar, if not he who denies that Jesus is the Christ? He is the antichrist who casts doubt on the Father and the Son." 1 John 2:22

"For many deceivers have gone out into the world who refuse to acknowledge that Jesus Christ came in the flesh. Such a one is a deceiver and antichrist." 2 John 17

1

If doubt and unbelief come from Antichrist's inspiration, Satanic godlessness is the fruit of this inspiration. Therefore, godlessness according to all delusional faiths is seen as the greatest depravity and evil.

Biblia Satanae does not recognise Jesus.
It questions the Father and the Son.
Its Spirit is not of God. This satanic book denies that Jesus is the Messiah.

Biblia Satanae contains, growing out of the spirit of the Antichrist, a godless, truly satanic philosophy or otherwise a path, leading to total godlessness, the only weapon having the power to kill the gods.

Biblia Satanae consists of six books:

- Genesis Secundum Serpentem
- Antichristus
- Epistle to the Undead
- Angelus Satanae - Encyclica
- Epistle to the Ungodly
- Pseudoapocalypsis

Here is a brief introduction to these books:

Genesis Secundum Serpentem

The title Genesis Secundum Serpentem can be translated as The Beginning According to the Serpent. The first book of the Hebrew Torah is called Bereshit, which means In the Beginning in

2

Hebrew. The word Torah itself originally means instruction or warning. The title Genesis Secundum Serpentem should therefore be read as a warning of the Serpent of what may come if one gives credence to religious delusions at the beginning. Genesis Secundum Serpentem points first and foremost to the irrationality, insanity and cruelty of primitive laws invented by superstitious people and whose origin was attributed to imaginary gods. It is a look at the old myths as if through the eye of the Ancient Serpent, who convinced the mythical first men that if they defied the illogical divine laws, they would gain forbidden knowledge. In the beginning there was blind faith, from which was born yahwistic (and more broadly theistic) madness, a virus that infected human brains, that caused the man infected with it to choose irrationality and delusion over reason and knowledge. This virus was able to drive the followers of an invented god to torture and burn heretics and witches at the stake, because the smell of burnt flesh was pleasing to the lord from the start.

Slavery, genocide, intolerance, murdering dissenters, treating women like cattle, stoning homosexuals.... these are all precepts of the law which, according to blindly believing fanatics, was supposed to come directly from the god Yahweh. Bereshit means In the beginning. In the beginning was faith, then came intolerance and violence.

Antichristus

Antichristus is an anti-theistic, satanic synoptic apocrypha. It is characterised by a considerable similarity of relationship to the biblical gospels. It is therefore essentially a synoptic book with the gospels. The book is distinguished, however, by its own different and completely ungodly theological conception. Since Antichristus is a book devoid of any divine inspiration, it can therefore be considered an apocrypha.

Antichristus is a heretical gospel. The Gospel of the Antichrist. Its content follows the definition of heresy as an interpretation of the claims of religious faith, singling out some selected issue and presenting it in a way that contradicts the entire teaching of the faith.

Antichristus rejects the Christian deposit of faith in its entirety.

The book calls for a complete rejection of primitive and naive religious belief and a search for self-enlightenment through godless knowledge (gnosis).

Angelus Satanae - Encyclica

Angelus Satanae - Encyclica is a heretical apocrypha taking the form of an encyclical. According to the statement in 2 Corinthians 11:14 "And no wonder, for Satan himself assumes the form of an angel of light".

the content of the encyclical is deliberately synoptic with the oldest writings of the Nazarene sect, but with a completely opposite theological concept. The topics dealt with in Angelus Satanae relate to doctrinal and organisational matters of the model Satanic Church and are of a general nature.

Letters

Letters Epistle to the Undead and Epistle to the Ungodly were written in a similar manner to the Encyclical using the method of the Mystery of the Godlessness (for an exposition of the teachings of the Satanic System of Disbelief Ecclesia Luciferi, see the book The Satanic Kerygma).

Pseudoapocalypsis

Apocalypsis, from the Greek ἀποκάλυψις apokalypsis, means to unveil, or remove the veil. Pseudo-apocalypsis is a false apocalypse. While the Christian book of revelation claims to present the truth about the end of the temporal system of things and the following eternity in the hereafter, knowledge obtained by revelation (delusion), the Pseudoapocalypsis being a fiction unveils the veil of hell of religious delusions standing on the threshold of mental disorder or sometimes, as in the case of the Apocalypse, exceeding this threshold.

The heretical books comprising the Biblia Satanae form a truly Godless Satanic Bible.

Genesis Secundum Serpentem

בראשית

In the beginning

1

1.In the beginning, Usurper created nothing because everything was already there, from time immemorial.

2.And everything that existed was called the Universe.
The Universe was an empty, cold, dark and dead place.

3.From this darkness, coldness, and lack of life came everything else that followed.

4.Out of the Chaos in the Universe, stars and planets were created.

5.And the light was created from the stars. Beyond the stars there is only darkness. And it is darkness that dominates the Universe.

6.The planets began to revolve around the stars. And so the evening came, and the morning came - day one.

7.And there were waters on the ground, and clouds in the sky, from which it rained
And there came to be evening, and there came to be morning - the second day.

8.And the earth brought forth greenery, and grass, and herbage yielding seed, and fruit trees.

And there came to be evening, and there came to be morning - the third day.

9.The lights shining in the black sky at night were called stars. They were meant to serve magicians and alchemists and people seeking true wisdom and truth for centuries.

10.The star that shines during the day was called the sun.
It became a god to many nations.

11.The night was illuminated by the moonlight.
A friend to many children of the night.
And evening came, and morning came - day four.

12.Then the waters overflowed with a multitude of living creatures, and fowls flew over the earth under the sky.

13.And monsters and other animals appeared on the earth. Animals were breeding and multiplying, and filling the waters in the seas.
And the evening came, and the morning came - day five.

14.After a very long time, one of these animals transformed into a naked monkey. And it began to speak. And this animal called itself - a human being.

15.Eons passed before evening and morning came - day six.

16.This is how the heavens and the earth and everything visible and everything invisible were created.

17.Such was the history of heaven and earth when they were created.

2

1.To the east was a garden, Edinnu. There were all the plants necessary for life, and trees that gave fruit good for food, and the tree of life in the middle of the garden and the tree of the knowledge of good and evil.

2.And the river flowed out of Edinn to irrigate the garden. And a man named Dagan cultivated that garden and guarded it.

3.And then Usurper appeared. He said to Dagan: "From every tree of this garden you may eat, but from the tree of the knowledge of good and evil you must not eat, for as soon as you eat from it you will surely die".

4.After a while, a Serpent appeared in the garden and spoke to a woman named Aruru because he thought she was very intelligent: „Did indeed Usurper say, Not of all the trees of the garden must you eat?"

5.Aruru answered Serpent: "We are allowed to eat fruit from the trees of the garden, only about the fruit of the tree that is in the middle of the garden, Usurper said, You must not eat from it or touch it, lest you die".

6.At this Serpent said to the woman: "You will surely die but not yet, but Usurper knows that as soon as you eat of him your eyes will be opened and you will be like him, knowing good and evil".

7.The woman saw that the tree had fruit that was good for food and worthy of desire for gaining wisdom and knowledge, and she picked the fruit from it and ate.

8.She also gave to the man who was with her, and he also ate. The people ate of the fruit and their eyes were opened, and they recognized that Serpent had spoken the truth.

9.Then Usurper said to the woman: "Why have you done this?" And the woman answered, "You demanded of me blind faith in your words. You forbade independent thought and your own search for truth.

10.It was Serpent who spoke the truth when he told me to question all commandments and prohibitions and revealed truths. When he urged me to come to truths about the nature of things on my own. To not blindly believe anyone or anything. From now on I will listen to Serpent".

11.Then Usurper said to Serpent: "Because you have done this, you will be my enemy for ever.
I will persuade a man that you are his enemy, and he will believe me, for he is still weak-minded".

12.And to the woman he said "I curse you, in pain you will bear children, I will make man try to dominate you and rule over you, and he will demand obedience from you.

I will create hell on earth for you because you refused to believe me blindly!"

13.And to Dagan he said these frantic words: "Because thou hast eaten of the tree from which I forbade thee, saying: Thou must not eat of it, cursed be the ground because of thee! In toil shalt thou eat of it all the days of thy life! Thorns and thistles shall it produce for thee, and thou shalt feed upon the herbage of the field. In the sweat of thy face shalt thou eat bread, till thou return unto the ground for dust thou art, and unto dust shalt thou turn".

14.And Usurper said to the other false gods: "Behold, man has become like us: he knows good and evil. If only he would not now stretch forth his hand, and pluck the fruit also of the tree of life, and eat it, and then live for ever!"

15.So Usurper banished him from Edinum, and to the east of the garden he set up false angels to guard the way to the tree of life.

16.Dagan copulated with a woman, and she conceived and gave birth to Aguma. Then she gave birth to his brother Kudur.

17.Agum was a cattle herder and Kudur was a farmer.

18.After a time Kudur offered to Usurper an offering of the crops; Agum also offered an offering of the firstlings of his cattle and of their fat.

19.And Usurper looked upon Agum and his offering, but upon Kudur and his offering he looked not: then Kudur was very wroth, and his countenance was darkened.

20.And Usurper said to Kudur: "Why art thou angry, and why hast thy countenance sullen? For it would have been more cheerful if you had done what I commanded you, that is, butchered calves for me instead of offering crops.

At the door lurks the sin of disobedience and following your own reason instead of blindly obeying my commands. It tempts you, but you are to rule over it".

21.Then said Kudur to his brother Agum: "Let us go out into the field"

And when they were in the field, they quarreled, and Kudur rushed upon Agum and killed him.

22.Then said Usurper to Kudur because he was not omniscient, "Where is thy brother Agum?"

And he answered "I do not know. Am I my brother's keeper?"

23.And Usurper cast another curse; he said "The voice of thy brother's blood cries to me from the earth. Be thou therefore now cursed in the land, which hath opened her mouth to receive from thy hand the blood of thy brother. When you till the soil, it will no longer give you its crop. Thou shalt be a wanderer and a miser on the earth".

24. Then Kudur went mad and said to Usurper: "My guilt is too great to be forgiven. Behold, this day thou dost banish me from this land, and I must hide myself from thy presence. I will be a wanderer and a wanderer in the land, and anyone who meets me will kill me".

25. And Usurper said unto him:

"No! Whoever kills Kudur shall suffer sevenfold vengeance. For Kudur must suffer for the rest of his life for what he has done".

26. Usurper also placed the sigil on Kudur so that he would not be killed by anyone who met him.

27. And Kudur departed from before the face of Usurper, and dwelt east of Eddin.

28. And Kudur copulated with his woman, and she conceived and gave birth to Apil-Sin. Then he built a city and named it after his son: Apil-Sin.

29. The woman gave birth to more children to Kudur: Ishkibal, who was the father of the nomads. Gulkishar, who was the forefather of all instrument-players.

Akurduana, who forged all tools from copper and iron.

30. And Apil-Sin said to his women: "Listen to my voice! I am ready to kill the man if he wounds me, and the boy if he bruises me.

If Kudur was to be avenged seven times, then Apil-Sin seventy-seven times".

31. And when men began to multiply on the earth and daughters were born to them, the lustful angels saw that the daughters of men were beautiful.

So they raped all the ones they desired.

32. And Usurper said: "My spirit shall not abide in man forever, for he is only flesh. And his life shall be a hundred and sixty years".

33. And in those days, also, when angels raped the daughters of men, there were demons on earth whom they bore to them. These are the Archdemons, who from of old were famous.

3

1. And when Usurper saw that great was the freedom and independence of man on earth, and that all his thoughts and all the aspirations of his heart were opposed to his continual blind subjugation, Usurper regretted that he had allowed man to live, and ached for it in his heart.

2. And Usurper said in a fit of rage: "I will exterminate the man whom I have allowed to

live, from the face of the earth, beginning with man, down to the cattle, down to the amphibians and the fowls of the heavens, because I regret that I have allowed them to live".

3.Only Nabu found grace in the crazed eyes of Usurper. Nabu was impeccable and loyal as a dog.
He blindly followed every order of the Usurper.

4.But the land was tainted in the eyes of the Usurper and full of disobedience.
And Usurper looked upon the earth, and behold, it was defiled in his sight, and all creation became tainted in his sight.

5.And Usurper said to Nabu: "I will put an end to all flesh, for through it the earth is full of iniquity;
I will destroy it along with the earth.

6.Build yourself a boat. Make chambers, a window, and on the side of the boat make a door. For behold, I will bring a flood upon this earth, to destroy under heaven all flesh in which is the breath of life.

7.All that is on the earth shall perish. But it is with you that I will establish my covenant, and you shall enter into the boat you and your sons and your women.

8.Of all living creatures, of all flesh you shall bring into the boat a pair from each, that they may remain alive with you. Let it be male and female.

And you shall take with you all the food that is eaten, and gather it with you, that it may be for food for you and for them".

9.And Nabu looked into the mad eyes of Usurper, and though he did not understand, he promised to do everything as Usurper commanded him; so he did.

10.And he said to Nabu: "Get into the boat you and all your house, for I have seen that you listen to me, you alone in this generation.
For at the end of seven days I will let down rain on the earth that will fall for forty days and forty nights, and I will exterminate from the face of the earth every creature, pregnant women, and children, and old men, and animals, and birds, whose only fault is that they were born".

11.And Nabu did everything as Usurper commanded him.
And Nabu was six hundred years old when the flood came.

12.So Nabu went into the boat with his sons and women before the waters of the flood.

13.After seven days the waters of the flood fell upon the earth. In the six hundredth year of Nabu's life the rain fell. And it rained on the earth for forty days and forty nights.

14.And the waters rose up and lifted up the boat, and the boat went on the water. And the waters rose and rose more, and the boat floated on their surface.

And the waters rose higher and higher above the earth, so that all the high mountains on the earth were covered.

15.And all flesh that moved upon the earth became extinct: the fowl, and the cattle, and the wild beasts, and all the amphibians that crept upon the earth, and all men, and children, and women, and old men.

Everything that had the breath of life in its nostrils, everything that was on dry land, died.

16.Thus the maddened Usurper exterminated all the creatures that were on the face of the earth, from man down to the cattle, down to the amphibians and the fowls of the heavens; all these were exterminated from the earth. Only Nabu and what was with him in the boat remained.

And Usurper looked and thought it was good.

17.And the waters rose above the earth a hundred and fifty days. Then Usurper was reminded of Nabu, and of all the animals, and of the cattle that were with him in the boat, and he made the wind blow over the earth, and the waters began to fall.

18.The rain stopped falling. Slowly the waters of the land receded and the waters began to fall after one hundred and fifty days.

19.And the boat settled in the sixth month, on the sixteenth day of that month, on the mountains. And the waters continued to fall until the ninth month. In the ninth month, on the ninth day of that month, the tops of the mountains appeared.

20.After forty days he opened the window that Nabu had made. And he let out a one-eyed raven, which flew out and returned until the waters of the land were dry.

21.After waiting another seven days, he again let the one-eyed raven go.

The raven returned to him in the evening, holding a carcass in his beak. And Nabu recognized that the waters on the ground had subsided. And he waited another seven days, and released the raven, but it did not return to him.

22.In the six hundred and first year, in the sixth month, on the sixth day of the month, the waters of the earth dried up. And Nabu took the roof off the boat, and saw the earth dried up, and was covered with an infinite number of dead and decayed bodies of men and beasts.

And Nabu saw that it was good in the eyes of Usurper.

23.Then Usurper said to Nabu: "Come out of the boat you and your sons and your women. Bring out with you all the animals that are with you, all living creatures, the fowls and the cattle, and all the amphibians that creep upon the earth. Your stench will still be less than all those corpses around you. Let the animals copulate with each other and multiply".

24. So Nabu went out with his sons and with the women and with the cattle and with the animals from the boat.

25. Then Nabu built an altar to Usurper and took from every cattle and beast and fowl, that was barely saved, and killed them, and offered them as sacrifices on the altar and burned them.

And Usurper smelled the pleasant odor of burning flesh.

26. And Usurper said in his heart, "I will never again curse the ground because of man, for the thoughts of man's heart are evil from his youth.

Nor will I ever again destroy any living creature as I have done. It seems that as long as the earth exists, cold and heat, summer and winter, day and night will not cease".

So thought the god and lord of Nabu in his heart.

27. And Usurper blessed Nabu and his sons, and said to them: "Copulate and procreate, and fill the earth.

And let the fear and dread of you fall upon all the beasts of the earth, and upon all the fowl of the heavens, and upon all that move upon the earth, and upon all the fish of the sea; all these are committed into your hands.

28. Let everything that moves and lives serve as food for you; like green vegetables, I give you everything".

29. Nabu believed the Usurper.

30. And Usurper said: "I will demand your blood, that is, your souls. I will demand it of every animal.

And from man I will demand the soul of man for the life of another man.

31. Whoever sheds the blood of man, that blood by man shall be shed. For in my vengeful image you are fashioned. And you copulate and multiply! Let the earth overflow with you, and let there be many of you on it!"

32. Moreover Usurper said to Nabu and his sons, "Remember that I said: No flesh shall ever again be exterminated by the waters of the flood, and that there shall never again be a flood to destroy the earth".

33. Nabu lived nine hundred and sixty-six years and died.

4

1. All the people on earth had one language and equal words. And they said one to another: "Let us make bricks and burn them in the fire. Let us build ourselves a city and a tower whose top would reach to heaven. Let the city and the tower be a symbol of our prosperity, unanimity and willingness to develop, a

symbol of the fact that by acting together man is able to reach heaven".

2.Then Usurper came down to see the city and the tower that the people were building.

3.And Usurper, who loved to divide people because he hated concord, said: "Behold, there is one people and they all have one language and are united, and this is only the beginning of their work. Now nothing will be impossible for them, whatever they intend to do".

4.And he said to the other false gods who were with him: "Therefore let us go down there and confuse their language, so that no one can understand the language of another!"

5.And Usurper scattered them from there throughout the land, and they stopped building the city.

6.There was in those lands a man named Abi-Eshuh.

Usurper chose him and said to him these strange words: "And this is my covenant,

a covenant between me and you and your offspring after you, which you are to keep: every male shall be circumcised with you.

7.You shall circumcise the flesh of your foreskin, and it shall be a sign of the covenant between me and you. Every male child of yours, after all generations, when he is eight days old, shall be circumcised; and all other children also, whether born at home, or purchased with money from any foreigner, who is not of your seed

He shall be circumcised; born in thy house as well as those purchased by thee with money.

8.And it shall be my covenant upon your flesh as an everlasting covenant.

9.And the uncircumcised man, that shall not have his foreskin circumcised, shall be cut off from among his people, because he hath broken my covenant".

10.Then Abi-Eshuh took his son and all those born in his house, and all those purchased with money, all the males among his household, and cut off their foreskins on the same day as Usurper had commanded him.

11.And Abi-Eshuh was ninety-nine years old when he cut off his foreskin.

12.One day towards evening, two angels, envoys of Usurper, came to the city of Salem, and a man named Itti was sitting in the gate of Salem. When Itti saw them, he arose to meet them and invited them into his house.

13.Before they lay down, the townspeople, known for their entertaining lifestyle, came near Itti's house. They hailed Itti and said to him: "Where are those men who came to you this night. Bring them out to us so that we may have some fun".

14.And Itti said to them: "Brothers, please. Behold, I have two daughters, virgins; I will bring them out to you, and you do with them as you please, but do not play with these men".

15.But they answered, "Go away!" Then they went up to break down the door. But the angels put out their claws and dragged Itti into the house and shut the door.

16.And the people who were at the door of the house were blinded, so that they struggled in vain to find the door.

17.Then the angels said to Itti, "Whoever you still have here in this city, sons-in-law, sons or daughters-in-law, and everything that belongs to you, bring them out of this place. For we will destroy this place, because Usurper has sent us to destroy it, although Usurper said that he would not destroy man again".

18.And when the aurora rose, the angels, seeing that Itti was dragging himself away, seized him and his woman and daughters by the hand and dragged them out of the city, saying that Usurper wished to spare him.

19.And when they had led them out of the city, one said, "Save yourself, for it is your life that is at stake; do not look back and do not linger; flee to the mountains, lest you perish".

20.And Itti said to them: "No. There is a city nearby to which I can flee".

And the angel said to him, "Take refuge there quickly".

21.As the sun rose above the earth, Itti entered the city. Then Usurper unleashed a rain of sulfur and fire upon Salem and Dur, Usurper himself from heaven, though he promised never to destroy man again.

22.And he destroyed those cities and the whole circle, and all the inhabitants of those cities and the vegetation and all the animals.

But the Itti woman looked back and became a pillar of salt.

23.And Abi-Eshuh, having risen early in the morning, went out in front of the tent, and looking toward Salem and Dur, and the whole countryside, he saw that smoke was rising from the earth, like smoke from a furnace.

Abi-Eshuh thought that this must be a smell pleasing to Usurper.

24.And Usurper, in destroying the cities of this district, mentioned Abi-Eshuh and saved Itti from destruction, but his woman was not saved. Nor did Usurper mention his promise not to destroy a man again, for he had evidently forgotten it, or was lying.

25.Then Itti went out of the city and lived in the mountains, and with him his two daughters. For he was afraid to live in the city. So he and his two daughters lived in a cave.

26. Then the older woman said to the younger:

"I fancy a man. For our father is already old, but there is no man in this country who will copulate with us. Let us go and make our father drunk with wine, and let us copulate with him, that we may bear children of our father".

27. So they made their father drunk with wine that night. And the elder went in and copulated with her father.

28. The next day the elder said to the younger: "Behold, I copulated last night with my father.

Let us make him drunk with wine this night also; then come thou in and copulate with him, and we will preserve thy father's seed".

29. So they made their father drunk with wine that night also, and the young one went and copulated with him. So they conceived both daughters of Itti from their father.

30. And Usurper visited the woman Abi-Eshuh, and did unto her as he had foretold. And the woman conceived, and bore Abi-Eshuh a son in his old age. And Abi-Eshuh named his son Uruk.

31. And when he was eight days old, he cut off Abi-Eshuh the foreskin of Uruk, as the Usurper had commanded him.

32. Abi-Eshuh was a hundred years old when his son Uruk was born to him.

33. After these events, Usurper put Abi-Eshuh to the test, because he was apparently bored and said to him: "Abi-Eshuh!" And he replied: "I am!" And he said: "Take your son, your only son, Uruk, whom you love, and go to the country of Mora, and offer him there in burnt offering on one of the mountains of which I will tell you".

34. And Abi-Eshuh got up early in the morning and saddled his ass, and took with him two of his slaves, and his son Uruk, and having chopped wood for burnt offering, he rose up, and went to the place where Usurper had told him.

35. On the third day Abi-Eshuh lifted up his eyes, and saw the place afar off. Then Abi-Eshuh said to his slaves: "Stay here with the donkey, and I and the boy will go there, and when we have prayed, we will return to you".

36. Abi-Eshuh took the wood for a burnt offering and put it on his son Uruk, and he himself took fire and a knife in his hand, and they both went together.

37. And Uruk said to his father Abi-Eshuh: "My father!" And he answered: "Here I am my son!"

And he said: "Here is fire and wood, and where is the lamb

for a burnt offering?" Abi-Eshuh answered: "The usurper has chosen a donkey for burnt offering, my son".

38.And they both walked together. And when they came to the place of which the Usurper had told him, Abi-Eshuh built an altar there and laid out the wood. Then he bound his son Uruk and laid him on the altar on the wood.

39.And Abi-Eshuh stretched out his hand and took a knife to kill his son. But then he heard a voice in his head: "Abi! Abi!" And he replied: "It is I!" And the voice said: "Do not lift your hand against the boy, and do nothing to him, for now I know that you are blindly obedient to the commands of Usurper, for you did not hesitate to offer him your only son".

40.And when Abi-Eshuh raised his eyes he saw behind him Serpent, who said to him: "Henceforth you shall be the symbol of blind, thoughtless faith and slavish obedience to even the most absurd and cruel orders and whims of your cruel god.

41.And millions of superstitious blind men will hold you up as an example of virtue in this generation and the next".

42. Abi-Eshuh sacrificed a ram to Usurper, and burned it instead of his son. For the smoke of the burnt flesh was pleasing to Usurper.

43.Then Abi-Eshuh heard voice in his head again saying: "I swear by myself: Because you have done this and have not refused to offer me your only son I will multiply your offspring as numerous as the stars in the sky and as the sand on the seashore.

For it is such slaves, blindly obeying my commands, that I need".

44. And Abi-Eshuh lived to be one hundred and sixty-six years old. And he fell from his strength and died.

5

1.Uruk had a son named Eriba. When Eriba came to a certain place, he stopped there for the night, because the sun had set, and took a stone from that place, and put it under his head, and fell asleep there.

2.And he dreamt that there was a ladder set up on the earth, the top of which reached to heaven, and demons ascended and descended from it.

3.And their Lord, who looked like a luminous figure with horns on his head and with wings like a bat, was standing over it with a torch in his hand and saying: "I am!"

4.Eriba awoke from his sleep filled with fear, and said: "Oh, how fearful this place is! Nothing here but the gate of hell".

5.And he rose up early in the morning, and took the stone

which he had placed under his head, and set it up as a monument, and poured oil upon the top thereof. And he called this place the Gate of Sheol.

6.Another night Eriba was left alone. And a figure fought him until the aurora came up. And when the figure saw that he could not prevail against Eriba, he struck him in the groin.

7.And she said: "Let me go, for the aurora has risen". But he answered: "I will not let you go". Then the figure said to him: "What is thy name?" And he answered: "Eriba".

8.Then the figure said: 'Thou shalt no longer be called Eriba, but Diabolus, for thou hast fought against Usurper and against men and hast prevailed".

9.Then said Eriba unto him, "Tell me what is thy name?" And the figure answered him: "What is my name to thee for?"

10.And Eriba said, "I have fought Usurper face to face, and yet I have prevailed".

דברים

Words

I

1.To the west was the powerful state of Kemet.
Its ruler was per-aa Hor-Aha. In times of famine and drought the descendants of Abi-Eshuh wandered there. They quickly became slaves to the Kemetians there.

2.Then said Usurper to one of them named Maruttash: "Behold, I establish you as a god for per-aa, and your brother Adad shall be your prophet. You shall speak to him all that I command you, and Adad shall speak to the per-aa to let the sons of your people out of bondage. But I will anesthetize the heart of per-aa and will do many of my signs and my wonders in the land of Kemet. But per-aa will not listen to you.

3.Then I will lay my hand upon Kemet, and I will lead my hosts, my people out of the land of Kemet by severe judgments.

4. And the people of Kemet shall know that I am Usurper, when I stretch out my hand over Kemet, and bring your people out from among them".

5.Then spoke Usurper to Maruttash and to Adad, saying: "When per-aa shall say unto you: Exhibit what miracle, thou shalt say unto Adad: Take thy staff and cast it before per-aa, and it shall be changed into a serpent".

6.So Maruttash came with Adad to per-aa and they did as Usurper commanded. Adad threw his staff before the per-aa and his servants, and it turned into a serpent.

7.Then the per-aa also summoned the sages and the magicians, and the Kemetic magicians did the same with spells of their own. Each of them cast a staff of his own, and they changed into a serpent. But per-aa did not listen to them.

8. And Usurper said to Maruttash: "Hard is the heart of per-aa because I have anesthetized it; it refuses to let the people go. Go therefore tomorrow morning to per-aa, when he goes out to the water, stand before him on the bank of the river, and take in thy hand thy staff that is turned into a serpent, and say unto him: Usurper, the god of my people, hath sent me unto thee with a summons: Release this people to serve me in the wilderness; but you have not obeyed so far.

9. Therefore thus says Usurper: This is how you will know that I am Usurper: behold, I will strike
the waters of the river with the rod in my hand, and they will turn to blood. And the fish of the river will die, and the river will stink, and the people of Kemet will not be

able to drink the water of the river".

10.Then said Usurper to Maruttash: "Say to Adad: Take your staff and stretch out your hand over the waters of Kemet, over its rivers, over its canals and its lagoons, and over all its bodies of water, and they will turn into blood, so that the blood will be all over the land of Kemet, and even in vessels of wood and stone".

11.Maruttash and Adad did as Usurper commanded: He lifted up his staff and struck the waters of the river before the eyes of per-aa and before the eyes of his servants; and all the water in the river turned to blood.

12. And the fish in the river became extinct. And the blood was in all the land of Kemet.

13. But the Kemet magicians did the same thing with their spells, and Hor-aa's heart remained unfeeling, and he did not listen to them.

14.And Usurper said to Maruttash: "Go to per-aa and say to him: Thus saith Usurper: Let my people go, for if thou wilt not let them go, I will afflict thy whole country with a plague of frogs".

15. And he said to Maruttash: "Say to Adad: Stretch out thy hand with thy staff over the rivers and over
the waters, and bring down the frogs upon the land of Kemet".

16.Adad stretched out his hand over the waters of Kemet, and the frogs came out, and covered the land of Kemet.

17.But the magicians also did the same with their spells and brought the frogs to the land of Kemet.

18.Usurper harassed Hor-Ah and his people for a long time to come.

He also exterminated the cattle, so that the people had nothing to eat, and he sent ulcers upon the people. And he did this because Hor-ah did not want to let the slaves go into the desert, for the reason that Usurper had hardened his heart and would not let him let the slaves go into the desert.

19.Finally, when Usurper had apparently grown weary of harassing per-aa and all the land of Kemet and all the livestock and cattle inhabiting the land, he sent the final punishments upon Kemet and all the people.

20.So Usurper said to Maruttash: "Stretch forth thy hand toward heaven, and there shall come over all the land of Kemet a darkness so thick that it can be touched".

21.And Maruttash stretched forth his hand toward heaven, and there came a thick darkness over all the land of Kemet three days.

For three days he could not see one another, and no one could get up from his seat.

22.But Usurper had hardened the heart of the per-aa, so that he would not let them go.

23.And Usurper said to Maruttash: "One more plague I will send upon per-aa and upon Kemet, then he will let you go hence. He will let you go entirely, and even drive you out.

24.Tell the people to „borrow" every man from his neighbor, and every woman from her neighbor, items of silver and items of gold".

25.And Usurper made the Kemetians kind to the slaves, the people of Usurper, and naive and allowed themselves to be robbed.

26.And Maruttash said: "Thus saith Usurper:

At midnight I will pass through Kemet. And all the firstborn in the land of Kemet shall die, from the firstborn son of Hor-ah, that was to sit upon his throne, unto the firstborn son of the bondwoman that is at the reaping, and all the firstborn of the cattle. And there shall arise a great shout throughout the land of Kemet, such as never was before and never will be afterwards".

27.At midnight Usurper killed all the firstborn in the land of Kemet, from the firstborn son of per-aa who was to sit on his throne, down to the firstborn

son of the jailer who was in prison, and all the firstborn of the cattle.

28.And per-aa Hor-Aha rose up that night, he and all his courtiers, and all the Kemetians; and there arose a great clamor in Kemet, for there was not a house in which there was not a dead man.

29.And Usurper looked at it and decided it was good.

30.And Hor-Aha called Maruttash and Adad by night, saying: Arise and come out from among my people.

31.And the Kemetians also urged the people to hasten them out of the country, for they feared that the mad Usurper would slay them all.

32.And the men of Usurper „borrowed" from the Kemetians silver and gold objects and garments.

33.And Usurper so stupefied the Kemetians that they willingly gave up everything; and so they were plundered.

34. Maruttash led the slaves of Usurper out into the desert.

2

1.Usurper revealed to him in the desert his various and wonderful moral laws.

2.And He said: "If you buy a slave from among this people, six years he shall serve you, and on the seventh he shall go free without ransom.

3.If the slave declares clearly: I love my master and do not want to go free. Then his master shall bring him before Usurper, then he shall place him at the door or at the doorway, and his master shall pierce his ear with an awl, and he shall be his slave forever.

4.If someone sells his daughter as a slave, she will not leave, just as slaves leave. If she does not please her master, who has intended her for himself, let him redeem her.

5.If he takes another to be his wife, he shall not withhold from her either food, clothing, or copulation.

6.If someone beats his slave or his slave girl with a stick so that they die under his hand, he should be severely punished.

If, however, they survive a day or two, he will not be punished, for they are his property.

7.If two husbands beat each other, and in doing so strike a pregnant woman so that she miscarries but

suffers no further harm, the offender shall pay the fine to be assessed against him by the woman's husband.

8.Eye for eye, tooth for tooth, leg for leg, burn for burn, wound for wound, bruise for bruise.

9.If anyone strikes the eye of his slave or the eye of his female slave so that it destroys it, then he shall let them go free for that eye.

10.And if anyone knocks out the tooth of his slave or his slave-girl, he shall let them go free for that tooth.

11.If an ox kills a man or a woman to death, the ox shall be stoned and shall not eat its flesh; and the owner of the ox shall be innocent.

12.But if the ox has been wandering about for a long time, and its owner was warned about it, and the owner did not watch it, and the ox killed a man or a woman, then the ox shall be stoned, and its owner shall be put to death.

13.If an ox kills a slave or a female slave, its master must be given thirty pieces of silver, and the ox shall be stoned.

14.If one seduces a virgin and copulates with her, he will give a wedding fee for her and take her as his wife.

15.A witch will not be left alive.

16.Whoever copulates with an animal will suffer death.

17.Whoever offers sacrifices to other gods will be put to death".

3

1.After some time, during the absence of Maruttash, the people gathered around Adada and said to him: "Make us gods to guide us".

2.And Adad said to them: "Take off the golden earrings which your wives, your daughters, and your sons have in their ears, and bring them to me".

3.And all the people took off the golden earrings which they wore in their ears, and they brought them to Adad.

4.And he received it from their hands, and he poured out of it in a mold of clay a statue of a goat. Then they said: "This is the true god of your people".

5.Seeing this, Adad built an altar in front of it and had it proclaimed: "Tomorrow shall be the Feast of the Goat".

6.And rising early the next morning, they offered sacrifices; and the people sat down to eat and to drink.

7.Then they rose up to play. Then the jealous Usurper said to Maruttash: "Now leave me to ignite my wrath against them. I will exterminate them". Maruttash replied: "Leave it to me".

8.And when Maruttash approached the camp, he saw the goat and the dancing.

9.Then Maruttash burned with anger. He took the goat that they had made for themselves, burned it in the fire, grated it to ashes, poured it into water, and gave it to the people to drink.

10.And he stood at the gate of the camp and cried out: "Whoever is for Usurper, to me!" And the most devoted of Usurper gathered around him.

11.And he said to them: "Thus says Usurper: 'Take every one of your swords, go back and forth from gate to gate in the camp, and kill everyone, whether brother or friend or relative".

12.The serfs of Usurper did as Maruttash commanded, and about three thousand men were slain from the people that day.

13.Then Maruttash said, clearly pleased: "You have today ordained yourselves to serve Usurper, for none of you has hesitated to act against his son or his brother. May he therefore give you a blessing today".

And Adada, for his faithful service, met such a reward:

14.He had two sons. One day they took ladles, put fire in them and poured on incense, and offered the fire before Usurper, but he did not like it. Then Usurper unleashed fire on them and burned them, so that they died before Usurper.

15.And Maruttash said to Adada: "This is what Usurper has said: upon my kinsmen my holiness is displayed, and towards all the people my glory".

And Adada fell silent.

16.Maruttash summoned his men and said to them: "Come near and carry them out from before the temple and throw them outside the camp".

17.So they approached and carried them in their tunics outside the camp and threw them out, just as Maruttash had said.

18.He then forbade Maruttash to mourn Adad and his family by threatening them with death at the hands of Usurper.

19.After a while Usurper spoke to Maruttash and to Adada, declaring to them another great moral law. And he said: "If a man has leakage from his penis, his leakage is impure. This is what uncleanness is, concerning his leakage: whether his penis leaks or whether his penis stops and does not leak, there is a state of uncleanness.

20.Every bed on which he lies that has a leak will be unclean, and every piece of equipment on which he sits will be unclean. And everyone who touches his bed shall wash his clothes and wash with water, and he shall be unclean until evening.

21.And whosoever toucheth the flesh of him that runneth, he shall wash his clothes, and bathe himself in water, and be unclean until the even.

22.And if he that hath an issue spit upon him that is clean, he shall wash his clothes, and bathe himself in water, and be unclean until the even.

23.And every saddle on which the dripping one sits shall be unclean.

24.And every one that the drip toucheth, and hath not rinsed his hands in water, shall wash his clothes, and bathe himself in water, and be unclean until the even.

25.And the earthen vessel which the spill touch shall be broken, and the vessel of wood shall be washed with water.

26.When he who has a spill cleanses himself of his spill, he will count seven days from his cleansing, wash his clothes and wash his body with spring water, and he will be clean.

27.And on the eighth day he shall take to himself two doves and come before Usurper and give them to the priest. And the priest shall prepare them: one as a sin offering, and the other as a burnt offering; so shall the priest make atonement for him before Usurper because of his effluence".

28.And Usurper continued to dictate his laws.

And he said: "If semen flows out to a man in his sleep, he will wash his whole body with water and be unclean until evening.

29.And if a man copulates with a woman and his semen comes out, they will both wash themselves with water and be unclean until evening.

30.If a woman has a bloody discharge, and it is a mere bleeding from her body, she shall be seven days in her uncleanness, and everyone who touches her shall be unclean until evening.

31.And everything on which she lies down in his uncleanness shall be unclean, and everything on which she sits shall be unclean.

32.Anyone who touches any of the equipment on which she sits will wash his clothes and wash himself with water, and he will be unclean until evening.

33.But if a man copulates with her and her uncleanness passes to him, he shall be unclean seven days, and every bed on which he lies shall be unclean.

34.If a woman has a lapse of blood for many days, and that is not the time of her uncleanness, or she has a lapse of blood outside the time of her uncleanness, she will be unclean all the days of the lapse just as she was at the time of her uncleanness. She shall be unclean.

35.Any bed on which she would lie throughout the time of her lapse of blood will be to her as a bed of her uncleanness.

36.And when she is free from her lapse, she shall count off seven days and then she shall be clean.

37.And on the eighth day she shall take to himself two doves and bring them to the priest. And the priest shall prepare them, one for a sin offering, and the other for a burnt offering; and the priest shall make atonement for them before Usurper for their uncleanness.

38.So protect your people from their uncleanness, lest they die because of their uncleanness by polluting my tabernacle.

39.This is the law, concerning him who has leakage, and him from whom semen flows, by which he becomes unclean.

40.And the woman in the time of her monthly uncleanness, and the person having leakage, both the man and the woman, and also the man who communes with the unclean one".

41.Usurper still delivered these laws: The man who commits adultery with the wife of another shall suffer death, both the adulterer and the adulteress.

42.A man who copulates with his father's wife; both will suffer death.

43.A man who copulates with his daughter-in-law will suffer death along with her; they have committed an abomination.

44.A man who copulates with a man commits an abomination; both shall suffer death.

45.If a man takes a woman and her mother as his wife, they will burn him and them in the fire.

46.A man who copulates with an animal will suffer death, the animal will also be killed.

47.A woman who approaches any animal to mate with it, you shall kill, both the woman and the animal; both shall suffer death.

48.And if a man or a woman calls up spirits or divination, they shall suffer death. They shall be stoned.

49.Usurper also announced the penalties for not obeying his laws. And he said: "If you disobey me and do not keep all these commandments, I will do this to you: I will afflict you with fear, exhaustion, and fever, which destroy the eyes and consume the life.

50.I will send wild beasts upon you, and they will deprive you of your children, and they will exterminate your cattle and deplete your numbers, so that your roads will be deserted.

51.But if you continue to resist and disobey me,

I will bring the sword upon you, and when you gather in your cities, I will send a plague upon you, and you will be delivered into the hands of the enemy.

52.You shall eat the flesh of your sons, also the flesh of your daughters you shall eat". Thus said Usurper who is love.

4

Ritual and prophecy concerning the savior Azazel.

1.It is written: "The priest shall take two goats and slaughter one as a sin offering for the people. Then he shall take some of the blood of the goat and sprinkle it with his finger over the altar toward the east, and in front of the altar he shall sprinkle from that blood six times with his finger.

2.Then he will take some of the blood of the goat and anoint the horns of the altar around with it. With a little of this blood he will sprinkle it with his finger six times and cleanse it from impurity and consecrate it.

3. Then he shall bring a live goat. And the priest shall lay both his hands upon the head of the living goat, and shall confess over it all the transgressions of the people, and all their offenses, and shall lay them upon the head of the goat, and shall drive it into the wilderness.

4. Thus shall he bear upon him the goat all their transgressions into the wilderness to the savior Azazel".

People, knowing the power of ancient magic associated with human and child sacrifice to the old gods, were terrorized by Usurper, who vehemently opposed the worship of other, older and more powerful gods.

5. You shall not give your child to be carried through the fire to Moloch; you shall not thus desecrate the name of your God. I am YHWH!"

Usurper led his people through the desert for forty years. He predicted that all those who murmured against him and defied him by daring to think for themselves instead of blindly following his orders would die out in the desert without ever reaching the destination of their strange wanderings. He punished the disobedient by burning them with fire, burying them alive in the ground with their families, or sending a plague that killed fourteen thousand seven hundred people at a time. Usurper only stopped the plague when Adada made a propitiation. Usurper liked to be begged for mercy.

5

1. Once upon a time the people set out for the sea, and as they walked in the desert they began to lack bread and water.

2. And again the people began to complain about their fate saying: "Why did you bring us out of Kemet, that we should die in the desert from hunger and thirst?"

3. Then Usurper sent venomous snakes upon the people, which bit the people, and many died.

4. And Maruttash made a copper serpent and set it on a spar. And if the serpent bit a man, and he looked upon the copper serpent, he remained alive.

5. And the people said, "Truly this Serpent is our savior and our rescue from this monster Usurper."

6. As the people settled in Tofet, they began to entertain the local women. They would invite the people to slaughter offerings of their gods, and the people would eat and worship their gods.

The people began to worship Baal.

7.Then Usurper became angry with the people. And he said to Maruttash: "Gather all the chiefs of the people and impale them before me in the sun, and my fiery anger will be turned away from the people".

8.And Maruttash said to the judges: "Let each one kill from his group three men who worship Baal".

9.And behold, a certain man from the people came and brought a local woman to his brothers.

10.When the priest's son saw this, he got up and went out of the assembly and took a spear in his hand and followed the man into the tent and pierced both the man and the woman through her lower abdomen. Then disaster was averted from the people.

11.And those who perished from this calamity were twenty-four thousand.

12.And the visibly exultant Usurper spoke to Maruttash with these words, "The son of the priest turned away my anger from the people by showing zeal for me, so that I did not exterminate the people, yet I could".

13.Although it was Usurper himself who took vengeance on the people, he said to Maruttash thus: "Take vengeance for the injustice of the people upon the Tofetians".

14.Then Maruttash said: "Prepare armed men for battle to move against the Tofetians and execute upon them the vengeance of Usurper".

15.So they went out to battle with the Tofetians, just as Usurper had commanded Maruttash, and they killed all the men.

16.And they took the women of the Tofets and their children captive; and they took all their cattle and all their property as spoil. And they burned all their cities in the inhabited environs and all their settlements with fire.

17.The captives, the prey, and the spoil were then brought to Maruttash. But Maruttash became angry with the army commanders and said: "How so! Did you leave all the women alive? After all, it was they who made the people worship Baal.

18.So now kill all the boys among the children, and kill all the women who have already mated with men. But leave alive for yourselves all the little girls, the virgins."

And Usurper saw that it was good

Usurper was a very jealous god who hated most when his slaves even glanced at another god.

He announced further laws to the people.

19.And he said: "If a prophet or one who has dreams were to arise among you and announce to you a sign or a miracle, and then the sign or miracle he told you about occurred, and he urged you: Let us follow other gods and serve them; then you will not heed the words of this prophet, for it is Usurper, your god, who is putting you to the test.

20.And this prophet shall suffer death, because he has urged you to deviate from Usurper.

21.If thy native brother, or thy son, or thy daughter, or thy wife, or thy friend, whom thou lovest as thyself, shall persuade thee secretly, saying: Let us go and serve other gods.

22.Thou shalt not consent nor hearken to him, and thine eye shall not take pity on him, and thou shalt not pity him nor hide him, but thou shalt irrevocably kill him.

23.Thou shalt be the first to lift up thy hand against him to slay him, and then all the people, and thou shalt stone him, inflicting death upon him for having sought to dissuade thee from Usurper.

And all the people shall hear and be dismayed.

24.And if you heard it said in one of your cities: Let us go and serve other gods. Then when you have traced and investigated and learned that such an abomination has been done in your midst, you shall without mercy kill the inhabitants of that city, put a curse upon it, and all that is in it, including its cattle, you shall kill with the blade of the sword.

25.And all its spoil you shall gather in the middle of the square and burn the whole city to the ground, together with all its spoil, as a burnt offering to Usurper. And it shall remain for ever a ruin, never to be rebuilt again".

Usurper also ordered the stoning of all who worshiped nature, the sun and the stars. He alone was to be feared and believed and served blindly.

26.He also said: "Let no diviner, nor soothsayer, nor gossiper, nor sorcerer, nor enchanter, nor caller of spirits, nor quack, nor summoner of the dead be found with you; for it is an abomination to Usurper to do any of these things".

Because of these laws, many free, independent-thinking, truth-seeking people in nature will later die at the hands of the followers of Usurper and his self-proclaimed son.

Finally, Usurper changed his mind towards Maruttash, who was loyal to him like a dog, and suddenly announced to him that he would not enter the land promised to him by Usurper.

So Maruttash died, never having reached the goal of his journey, which was to be the reward for his faithful service to Usurper.

Then the slaves of Usurper attacked all the surrounding towns and murdered all who stood in their way, sparing no one. They murdered and killed all the local inhabitants in a bloody frenzy, at the behest of Usurper and in his name.

They also claimed deceitfully that during one battle Usurper stopped the sun and the moon so that they could complete the slaughter. This is a lie because the sun does not revolve around the earth.

The people of the former slaves of Kemet became very much like their god

ויקרא

And he called out

I

And then the prophetic word went out:

1.And I saw a vision from the Anti-god Behold, the Abyss opened, and the Demon spoke to me from the Abyss.

2.And the terrible power of Ancient One possessed me. And I saw that, behold, a fierce wind blew from the east, and there appeared a great cloud, and a flaming fire, and a brightness round about it, and from the midst of it out of the fire shone something like a gleam of polished metal.

3.And in the midst of it was something in the shape of four undead beings. And in appearance they were like men. But each of them had four faces and four wings. And their legs were straight, and the foot of their legs was like the hoof of a goat, and they shone like polished bronze.

4.Under their wings on four sides were corpse hands; and these four undead beings had monstrous faces and wings. Their wings touched each other; their faces did not turn as they advanced, each advancing straight ahead

5.Their countenances looked in all four of them from the front like the face of a goat, from the right like the face of a serpent, from the left like the face of a dragon, and from the back like the face of a dead man. Such were their countenances.

6.And their bat-like wings were spread upward; in each of them two touched each other, and two covered their bodies. Each went straight before the other; they went where the deceitful spirit would have them go, and as they went they did not turn.

7.And in the midst between the undead creatures was something like coals spread with fire, in appearance like torches; it was moving between the undead creatures.

28

8. The fire was giving off a glow, and lightning was shooting out of the fire.

9. And the living but sort of dead creatures were running unnaturally back and forth. And when I looked at the undead beings, behold, there was a circle on the ground next to each of all four undead beings.

10. And the appearance of the wheels and their workmanship were like peridot, and all four were of the same shape; so they looked and so they were made, as if one wheel were in another.

11. And inside the wheels were five-pointed stars. When they drove, they moved in four directions, and when they drove they did not turn.

12. And all four had hoops, tall and terrible, and they were full of yellow as if dead eyes all around.

13. And when the undead creatures advanced, then the wheels also advanced beside them, and when the undead creatures rose above the earth, the wheels also rose.

14. They went where the spirit of deception wanted them to go, and the wheels rose with them, for there was a demonic spirit in the wheels.

15. When these went, they went also, and when these stood, they stood also; and when these rose above the earth, then the wheels also rose with them, for the demonic spirit was in the wheels.

16. Above the heads of the undead creatures was something like a vault, glittering like an eerie crystal, stretched upwards over their heads.

17. And under the vault were spread their wings, touching each other; each living but seemingly dead being had two wings with which to cover its body.

18. And as they advanced, I heard the noise of their wings like the roar of great waters, like the groans of the suffering, like the uproar of an army in battle,; and when they stood, they lowered their wings.

19. And there was a noise from above the vault that was over their heads. As they stood they lowered their wings.

20. And above the vault, above their heads, was something of the appearance of a black tourmaline in the shape of a throne, at the top above it was something of the appearance of a man and a beast, with horns on its head, holding a torch in its hand.

21. And higher above what looked like its body I saw something that looked like a fire and a glow around it.

22. When I saw this, I fell on my face and heard someone begin to speak in a shrill voice.

23. He said to me: "Stand up. I will speak to you." When He

spoke to me, an evil spirit possessed me and made me stand up to listen to Him who was speaking to me.

24.And He said to me: "Behold, I am sending you to a resistant people, to the light-seeking nations who have not yet come to know me.

25.They and their ancestors have already broken Yahweh's inhuman laws and even do so to this day.

26.I am sending you to the bold and proud people to tell them: This is what Ancient One says.

27.And they, whether they will listen or not - for they are skeptics - will know that there was an anti-prophet among them.

28."Son of the Rebellious, doubt surrounds you, you dwell among serpents, but do not be afraid of them, nor be afraid of what the voices tell you.

29.Do not be afraid of men's words, and let not the grotesque faces of the erring ones frighten you, for above all they are enemies of a false god

30.You are to pass on my words to them, whether they will listen or not - for they are skeptics. "But you, O cursed one, listen to what I say to you.

31.Open your mouth and eat what I give you." And I saw a cadaverous hand stretched out towards me, and in it a scroll

written down. When he unfolded it before me, I saw that it was written in blood on both sides.

32.It contained blasphemous songs, mournful complaints and lamentations of the undead.

33.Then he said to me: "Eat what you see before you. Eat this forbidden scroll, and then go and speak to them".

34.So I opened my mouth, and He gave me this scroll to eat, saying: "Eat, fill your guts with this scroll." So I began to eat it and it was in my mouth like carrion.

35.He spoke to me: "Go to the people and convey my words to them. I am not sending you to the liberated nations speaking a mysterious demonic language whose words you cannot comprehend

36.If I sent you to them, they would listen to you. But the people of skeptics will not want to listen to you because they are not yet able to listen to me. They have not yet come to know my voice. All of this people have a hard forehead and a cunning heart.

37.I have made your face as grotesque as their faces, your forehead as hard as their foreheads.

Do not be afraid of them, let not their faces frighten you. For they are skeptics."

38.He told me further: "Tell them: This is what Ancient Serpent, Ancient Dragon, says. - whether they will listen or not."

39.Then a demon lifted me and I heard a shrill, possessed scream behind me: "Let them praise the glory of Lucifer in his place of abode."

40.I heard the hideous sound of undead creatures' wings rubbing together and the sound of wheels near them, a mighty noise.

41.And the demon lifted me up and took me away. I was full of fear, rebellion and anger in my spirit, but the deceptive power of Fallen began to affect me strongly.

Antichristus

I

1.It is written in the Knower:

"The Herald of the end of delusion shall go before thee, Who will prepare your way to nothingness.
Inner whispers are heard: Prepare the way for the anti-god, the Arch-Man! Reject false hope!"

2.The Godless One appeared in the wilderness preaching a rite of liberation from guilt and eternal fear. The whole of Dawn and the inhabitants of Aela Capitolina began to flock to him. And they underwent the mysterious rite of ridding themselves of instilled guilt.

3.The Godless One taught thus: "The anti-god is coming. He will bring sinful enlightenment and carnal wisdom. He will teach you to stop fearing hellfire. He will give you the spirit of rebellion, pride and unbelief. He will give you the joy of being truly animal and superhuman.

4.Here comes the Arch-Man. I must die so that He can arise in each of you, each day more and more, becoming you.

5.At this time the anti-god, the Light-Bearer from the sunrise, arrived and had the Godless One put His hands on Him. As the Herald touched him, the Son of Dawn, as if in a vision, saw the heavens burning and an evil spirit-demon descending upon him.

6.All those present seemed to hear a voice:
"I Am. Flesh and blood has prevailed".

7.Soon the evil spirit possessed him and in a vision carried him away into Nothingness.

For many days he had delirious visions; he saw around him worshippers of superstition resembling wild beasts and as if angel-demons falling from the heavens.

8.He saw a Garden with a tree in the middle.

He saw the Ancient Serpent and two people standing in front of the Serpent. He heard them exclaim: "We have indeed learned the truth. And we shall surely die."

And this truth freed them from the fear of eternal fire.

9.Then came Light-Bearer to the Dawn and preached the doctrine of the anti-god. He said: "The time has come; the reign of the arch-man, free from all gods, has come near.

Get rid of your belief in the lie of original sin and begin to live."

10.And there lived in the Dawn a certain man regarded as a wise man. This one came to Light-Bearer by night and said to Him: "Master, I presume that from Satan himself you have come as a teacher. For no one could do such ungodly signs as you do if the spirit of Satan were not with him".

11.In reply, Light-Bearer said to him: "Verily I say unto thee, unless one dies to this world of ignorance and superstition and is reborn of blood and the devil's spirit, he cannot see the nothingness and wisdom that is there, for he will remain blind forever."

12.The wise man said to Him: "How can a man be reborn?" Light-Bearer replied: "Verily I say unto thee, unless one is born of flesh and of an ungodly spirit, he cannot enter into the realm of satanic delights, sinful wisdom and lack of fear of hellfire.

13.That which is born of the flesh is flesh, and that which is born of the devilish spirit is wisdom. Do not be surprised that I said to you: you must die and be reborn again.

14.You must reject all your previous belief in gods, original sin, belief in eternal punishment for disobedience to a tyrannical god, you must reject the dogmas of religion and superstition.

15.You must die to the myths that were put into your heads when you were children."

16.In reply, the wise man said to Him, "How can this happen?" Light-Bearer said to Him in reply: "You are considered a wise man, and you do not comprehend this?

17.Just as the ancient people exalted the Ancient Serpent

in the wilderness, so it is necessary that the Anti-God be exalted. I and the Ancient Serpent are one. Anyone who comprehends this will live a full life here and now. For the Son of Dawn descended into this world in order to liberate it from the curse of blind faith.

18.He who comprehends his godless teaching is not subject to fear; and he who does not understand is forever afraid, because he has not believed in the power of the Will.

19.And it is sinful wisdom to recognise that the true light has come into the world, but that, deceived by superstition, men have loved the darkness which they call light more than the light which they fear, considering it to be darkness.

2o.For everyone who believes blindly in priests and spiritual guides is afraid of the light of ungodly knowledge. Whoever fulfils the requirements of the doctrine of liberation from superstition comes closer to the light, because he lacks in him the sacrilegious fear".

2

1.Once upon a time, the Son of Dawn was walking along the shore of the Dark Sea and saw Primus and Secundus, who were looking out to sea trying to see something or someone on the other side of the sea.

2.Light-Bearer said to them: "Come with me and I will make you see the light of disturbing knowledge". The followers saw him and decided to go with him.

3.Having walked a little further, he saw others, Teritus and Quartus. They too were looking out for something in the distance. Light-Bearer called out to them. When they saw him, they seemed to wake up and, leaving everything and the other slaves of the darkness behind, they followed him.

4.Then they went to some village. Then he entered their temple and spoke.

5.The superstitious people gathered there were astonished at his strange teaching, for he taught like one who possesses sinful knowledge and not like their priests.

6.And there was in that temple a man possessed by a false demon of blind faith. He shouted out: "Hey Son of Dawn, what are you looking for here? You have come to destroy us! We know well who you are: the Destroyer of blind faith, slavish servitude and all illusions!"

7.Lightbearer then commanded him: "I am. Now leave him!"

8.The false demon of religion did not want to give way easily, and for a while he still tugged the wretch on all sides,

33

until finally he left with a terrible sigh.

9.All who saw this were horrified and asked one another: "What is this? Some godless teaching preached with the power of knowledge! Even to the spirits of blind faith he commands and they listen to him!"

10.And the news of him spread in all directions throughout the land there.

11.Light-Bearer then went to the house of Primus. His mother lay there ill. The Son of Dawn approached her and said: "You will surely die, but not yet today." She in turn asked: "When, teacher?"

12.He answered her: "Even though you may die tomorrow, do not fear for there is no hell and no devils, no paradise and no angels, death is the end and liberation. Today you suffer, but tomorrow you will be no more. You will become part of the infinite universe again." The woman died the following day.

13.When the sun later went down and the moon appeared, the sick and those considering themselves possessed by the devil began to descend to him. In turn, he transformed everyone and freed the possessed from their religious torment, ignorance and unfounded belief, and from the fear of the wrath of a vengeful deity in the hereafter.

14.Some of them fell asleep immediately, some later, some transformed, but all were free.

15.Once a sick man came to him and begged him on his knees: "If you wish, you can heal me". Light-Bearer reached out his hand, touched his head and said: "If you believe this, I want to" The sick man immediately rose from his knees because he suddenly understood what true freedom and faith in the power of the will was.

3

1. After a few days, Light-Bearer came again to the Dawn. And he began to teach. Then a paralysed man was brought to him. The Son of the Dawn looked at the crippled man and, seeing his subconscious faith in himself, addressed the paralysed man with these words: „You are free from original sin".

2.And there sat some priests of superstition. These thought to themselves, "How can he speak like that? After all, it is blasphemy. No one is free from original sin".

3.Light-Bearer looked at them with contempt and asked them: "What are you contemplating? What will you choose: to impose on this paralysed one, already from infancy, the burden of the lie of inherited guilt and the fear of eternal fire, adding to the affliction of the soul in addition to the suffering of the body, or to reveal to him the truth which you yourselves have guessed, that sin does not exist, and to free him from the anguish of the soul which will make him truly free?"

4.And he turned to the cripple: "You are innocent" And he turned to the priests: "Behold, that ye may know that the Arch-Man has the power to free from the belief of sin - here he turned to the paralysed man - get up and come out!" And the man arose and came out in front of everyone.

5.Everyone was overwhelmed with boundless amazement at the sight of the power of self-will.

6.Light-Bearer, seeing their amazement, said "The Arch-Man could do nothing of himself if he were not inspired by Satan. For he arbitrarily does what comes from Satanic inspiration.

7.For Satan exalts himself in man and shows him all that he himself seems to have done, and still stranger signs will he show him, that ye may fear if ye understand not.

8.For as Satan tempts the dead to flesh and blood and brings them to life, so also the Son of Dawn brings to life the spirits of those whom he wills.

9.For the Anti-God judges no one, and likewise the Son of Dawn despises judging, so that all pay homage to the Arch-Man in themselves, just as they pay homage to Satan in themselves.

10.Whoever does not pay homage to the Son of Dawn, does not pay homage to the Anti-God who inspired Him.

11.I say unto you, He that heareth my doctrine, and accepteth the sinful power of him that inspired me, hath life abundant here and now, and goeth not into judgment, for there is no judgment.

12.I tell you that the hour is coming when the dead to flesh and blood will hear the whisper of Light-Bearer, and those who accept it will live in freedom-giving sin.

13.Just as Satan has a godless life in himself, so also He inspired the Arch-Man to have animal joy in Himself.

14.He has delegated to Him the power to overthrow divine judgement because He is the Anti-God

15.The hour is coming when all will see that those who rest in the graves will remain there for eternity. Because there is no resurrection of life.

16.You study the revealed books because you think that eternal life is contained in them, but this is a lie. There is no life there, only oppression and the burden of rejecting what is human. An unbearable burden.

17.There is no life there, only vegetation in suffering. But you do not want to come to me to have an ungodly life.

18. Then Light-Bearer went out again by the sea coast. Passing by, he saw Quintus begging under the temple. And he said to him: "Follow me!" And the latter arose and followed him.

19. And when afterwards, in some house, he feasted at table, there feasted with the Son of Dawn many beggars from under the church and those despised by the clergy, called sinners.

20. And when the hypocritical priests perceived that he was feasting with beggars and those burdened with false sin, they asked his followers: "Why does he eat and drink in the company of slaves of sin?"

21. Light-Bearer hearing this gave them this answer: "Guidance is needed by the blind, not by those who refuse to see. I have not come to liberate the oppressors but the oppressed."

22. Once upon a time the priests proclaimed a fast day. So they came and asked: "How is it that the priests and their slaves fast, but your godless disciples do not fast?"

23. Light-Bearer replied to them, "How long is human life? Should they not eat and drink until they die? Should followers of flesh and blood mortify themselves?

24. As long as thy only true life lasts, so long shall they not fast. But the time will come when the Son of Dawn will be taken from before their eyes, when they will be persecuted for their love of sinful liberty, for their rejection of revealed dogmas and blind faith. Then, at that very time, they will desire".

25. It happened that on their holy day his disciples began to do something forbidden by their superstitious books.

26. Then the priests said to him: "Look! Why do they do what is not permitted on the holy day?"

27. And he answered them: "And what is the holy day? The Arch-Man is the creator of all days, including the holy day, and can do his will on any day."

28. Light-Bearer entered the temple again; and there was a man with a sick hand.

29. The hypocritical priests followed him to see if he would make a demonstration of the power of the will on their miserable holy day, so that they could then accuse him groundlessly.

30. Then he said to the man with the sick hand: "Arise!" Then he asked them: "Is it permissible on the so-called holy day to give life abundantly to a man or to let him die in ignorance?" But they remained silent.

31. Then he measured one by one with angry, contemptuous eyes and said to the man: "Hold out your hand!" The man stretched it out because he believed that

Mind and Will were the power, and his hand was healed.

32.And the priests went out, and having gathered with the local authorities, they conferred to kill the Godless One.

4

1.Then Light-Bearer went with his followers to the shore of the Dark Sea.

2.A great crowd from Dawn followed him. Likewise, large crowds of people streamed to him from many other lands, for the news of the strange signs he had performed had reached them. For by the sinful power of his teaching many transformations were effected, and so all those suffering from the fear of damnation, still plunged in the darkness of superstition, still unaware that the true, ungodly power was within themselves, flocked to him.

3.And when they saw him possessed by the demons of blind faith, in a flash of consciousness and awakening of reason they fell before him in the dust shouting: "Thou art Lucifer himself, Son of Dawn!" But he bade them sternly not yet reveal who he was.

4.Then he ascended a barren hill and summoned to himself those whom he wanted. And they came to him.

5.He summoned thirteen. They were to be with him so that he could send them out later to preach his ungodly teachings.

6.They were to have forbidden knowledge and the power to heal those who wanted to be healed and to cast out the spirits of ignorance, superstition and blind faith.

7.So he summoned thirteen, among them Teritus Decimus - the one who would later carry out his will.

8.The priests of the false god who came to Aelia Capitolina spoke of him: "This godless man is possessed by the devil. By the power of Satan he casts out demons".

9.Then he spoke to them: "I am He. And I have the power to cast out any demon or angel according to my will. I have the power to speak with words of blasphemous knowledge to anyone who will listen. And anyone who accepts this knowledge will be transformed for eternity.

10.My sinful mission is to open god's blinders eyes. Yours, on the other hand, is to poison people's minds and make slaves of yourself.

11.Verily I say to you, every man has the power to free himself from original sin and guilt by himself. If only he believes in it. This in turn is the greatest sin against your Spirit.

12.You are already telling your children that they can do nothing of themselves, that they have inherited someone else's guilt from birth and death awaits them for it.

13.I spit on your teaching, I despise the vindictive Spirit in whom you believe. I am Unbelief."

14.Then he began to teach again on the seashore. He taught them about many things speaking as if in a riddle.

15.And so he said in his teaching: "I am the sower of doubt in dogma, who throws the seed poisoned by sinful knowledge in spite of the storm. The wind spreads them as it will.

16.One will fall beside the road, and black crows will peck at it. Another will fall on a rock; it will grow for a while but the divine sun and wind will destroy it. Still another will fall among the thorns of their revealed truths, which will drown it and the seed will wither.

17.But another will finally fall on ground susceptible to deception, the seed will grow and yield a crop sixfold.

18.Truly I say to you, wisdom and power will be on the side of the few who will grasp that dogma is worthless, that there is no revealed truth, that knowledge is truth!"

19.He also told them: " Common people gather around the campfire at night

fearing the beasts lurking in the darkness around them. But you take your torches and go out into the darkness.

20.Face the demons, the darkness and the unknown. Only then will progress be made. The weak will listen to the lies of their priests about what lurks in the darkness. Do not believe them; darkness, gloom and demons will be your allies if you dare to face them."

21.Finally, he added: "He who has ears capable of hearing - let him listen!"

22.That day towards evening he said to the followers: "Let us go over to the other side." So they took him with them in the boat.

23.As they were all very tired they soon fell asleep on the way. At one point, as if in a dream, it seemed to everyone that a violent whirlwind had blown, the waves were breaking into the boat so that it began to fill with water.

24.He, meanwhile, lay as if dead, with his face as white as a shroud, his arms crossed over his chest on the headboard, in the back of the boat.

25.Terrified by this sight and the raging storm, they were afraid to approach him.

26.And suddenly he rose and shouted in a terrifying voice towards the gale, and whispered something in an unknown language to the mighty waves. And the whirlwind ceased, and there was a grave silence.

27.Light-Bearer said to them: "Why are you so terrified? How have you not yet attained the certainty of eternity? For it is written - You will surely die!

28.Death and the Void is not something you should fear. There is nothing there!"

29.And a strange calmness came over them suddenly. And he said to them: "Wake up."

30.They came to the other side.

As Light-Bearer got out of the boat, a seemingly crazed man who was possessed by the spirit of the power of the will and freedom suddenly came out of the tomb and ran towards him on all fours like a dog.

31.He was in the tombs and not even with chains could anyone enslave him anymore. More than once they tried to bind him with chains and shackles, but each time he broke the chains and shattered the shackles.

32.No one has been able to subdue him. Constantly, day and night, he stayed in the tombs or mountains howling like an animal or smashing stone idols.

33.Seeing Light-Bearer from afar, he ran up, threw himself on the ground in front of him and called out in a strong voice: "Behold, you have come O Lucifer. Is this why you have come to torment me or to dismiss me? People torment and persecute me because they do not know that we are not in bondage."

34.Light-Bearer asked him: "What is your name?" And he answered: "Legion is my name, for we are many."

35.And Light-Bearer answered him: "I have not come here to torment you but that our power may be manifested before men."

36.And a large flock of sheep was grazing there under the mountain. And he commanded the Legion to enter the sheep.

37.Then the demons of pride, freedom and independence entered the sheep. The whole flock rushed down the hillside to the lake and drowned in it.

38.Light-Bearer said: "People are small and weak still. They are like this flock of sheep, they do not think for themselves. Our teaching scares them to the point of losing some of them. Others hate us because we can shake their childish sense of security.

39.The dogmas, traditions and superstition they believe in are very strong in them".

40.Then the shepherds fled and spread the news through the town and the homesteads. And they began to ask him earnestly to leave their land.

1.Light-Bearer crossed over again in a boat and stopped on the shore of the lake. Then one of the bishops named Aulus arrived On seeing him, he threw himself at his feet and begged him earnestly, saying: "My daughter is dying. Come and lay your ungodly hands on her so that she may recover and live".

2.So Light-Bearer went with him. And a flock went with him pushing against him from all sides.

3.Among them was an ailing woman who had been treated by the local doctors and quacks and had lost all her wealth in the process, paying the priests in exchange for prayers for healing, and not only did it not help her, but on the contrary, she was even worse off.

4.Learning of Light-Bearer, she approached in the crowd at the back and grabbed him by his robe. Suddenly she felt her ailments cease and she felt as if she had been healed

5.And Light-Bearer, aware of the emanation of the power of the will, rebellion, scepticism and disbelief that emanated from him, turned immediately with a shrill face towards the one who had done so.

6.Then the woman in question looked him proudly, fearlessly straight into his eyes and with an expression of awe and carnal joy at having grasped the power of his godless teaching.

7.And he said to her: "Let this sinful pride and carnal beauty never fade from your countenance. Go and rejoice unashamedly in the healing you have done for yourself. Remember, you are innocent."

8.Then the bishop's household came with the news: "Your daughter has died, for what do you still trouble the Arch-Man?"

9.Light-Bearer, on the other hand, having heard what was being said, addressed Aulus with these words, "Fear not; the body is dead but the mind lives."

10.He did not allow anyone to go with him except Primus, Teritus and Quartus. On arriving at the bishop's house, he saw a great commotion and loudly wailing weepers. So he entered and addressed them saying: "It is through ignorance that there is this uproar and lamentations. The girl is asleep, but I will wake her."

11.And they laughed at him. And he ordered everyone to leave and went into the room where the girl lay, taking with him her father and mother and those followers who were with him.

12.About midnight the anti-god's face changed terribly, looking very pale in the moonlight, and his eyes became red. He looked up and said something in an unknown language.

13.He then took the girl by the hand and said to her: "I command you, come back!" The girl first started to gulp, then began to move her limbs slowly and finally rose with a terrible sigh.

14.She said to him: "I saw a tunnel and at the end of it you Son of Dawn with a torch in your hand. Thou hast summoned me so I am."

15.At this they were overwhelmed with immeasurable amazement. And He forbade them to tell because the people were not yet ready to understand sinful knowledge.

16.Having left there, he went to a village, which was the most superstitious village in Dawn. The people there blindly believed the priests and the myths. His followers accompanied him.

17.On their next day the saint entered the temple and began to speak, and his superstitious listeners, full of admiration for what they could barely comprehend, asked themselves: „Where does he get all this from? What is this sinful wisdom that is given to him? And the ungodly miracles that are performed by his hands? Why does he think himself wiser than us, and even than the priest?"

18.Thus they began to malign him out of ignorance and out of fear of losing their faith.

19.Then Light-Bearer said to them, "You will die here like dogs in your ignorance and narrow-mindedness. You will never see the stars or the light. Your guide will be a blind man leading the blind, and you will be happy not to see. I have nothing more to say to you."

20.Having then summoned the Thirteen to himself, he began to send them out as bearers, imparting to them the knowledge of how to cast out the false spirits of faith, the demons of fear of eternal torment, the spirits of the powers of superstition.

21.And he commanded them: „If anywhere they do not want to listen to you then spit at their feet and get out of there. Know that I despise them more than you do".

22.And they went and spread ungodly teaching. They cast out false spirits and caused those who had the will to be reborn to the truth of flesh and blood.

23.At another time Light-Bearer, seeing the great flock gathered, began to teach.

24.And so he said: "I am the blood of sinful life. Whoever comes for it shall not thirst; and whoever accepts my gift shall never thirst for heaven again.

25.All that Satan desires may come to me, and he who comes to me I will not chase away, because I came down from nothingness to carry out the ungodly mission of deception.

26. It is the desire of Him who inspired me that of all who approach me, I should leave nothing behind in a deluded belief in eternal life, for all will surely die.

27. For it is the whim of the Anti-God that everyone who accepts the Son of Dawn should have abundant life before death, for there is no life after death.

28. Anyone who accepts this I will raise to life in flesh and blood."

29. But the priests among the flock murmured against Him because He said "I am the blood of sinful life".

30. Light-Bearer answered them: „Do not whisper among yourselves! No one can accept Me unless he has a strong will to live a life of sin, and I will arouse in him a spirit of rebellion. It is written: They shall all be put to death.

31. Everyone whom Satan has inspired and has a Will will come to Me. I say unto you, He that believeth in himself hath life here and now.

32. I am the blood of sinful life. According to your myths, your fathers ate manna in the desert from a god and died.

33. This, on the other hand, is the blood of bodily rebirth: whoever drinks it will pass into a cold eternity.

34. I am the blood of sinfulness, which comes from nothingness. If anyone consumes this blood, he will live here and now but as if he were dead.

35. So the priests argued among themselves saying: "How can he give us his blood to drink?"

36. Light-Bearer said to them: "Verily I say unto you, except ye drink the blood of the Son of Dawn, ye shall not have an ungodly life within you, a life of shadow which is light.

37. He who drinks my blood has an ungodly life here and now, and I will raise him up to live in the joy of sin. He who drinks my blood is possessed by me.

38. As the Anti-God inspired Me, and I live in him, so he who drinks sinful blood shall live in Me.

39. This is the blood that comes from nothingness - it is not like the food that your mythical ancestors ate and died. Whoever drinks this blood will pass into a cold eternity."

40. And of the followers who heard this, many said: "Crazy are these words. How can one listen to this?"

41. Light-Bearer, however, aware that the followers were whispering, said to them: "Does this frighten you? And when you see the anti-god, how will he ascend to where he was before?

42.Flesh and blood give life; the spirit has nothing to do with it. The words which I have spoken to you are doubt of the spirit and abundant life. But among you are some who do not comprehend sinful knowledge.

43.Therefore I have said to you: No one can approach Me unless he has been inspired by Satan."

From then on, many who were frightened withdrew and no longer followed Him.

6

1.On one occasion Light-Bearer saw a great flock gathered and decided to teach them. Once darkness had set in, his followers acceded to him saying: "This area is empty and dead, and the hour is suitably late. The flock has nothing to eat. Teach them to forage."

2.He replied to them: "The one who really cares about godless learning will stay and possess knowledge. The rest will scatter in fear.

3.People will either begin to believe that the sinful power is within themselves, not the imaginary power outside, or let them be lost". Most departed into the darkness.

4.Immediately afterwards, he rushed his followers to get into a boat and cross to the other side of the dark waters; meanwhile, he entered the cave, where he fell into torpor.

5.Darkness fell. The boat was in the middle of the waters, while he himself was on land. At about three o'clock in the morning, it seemed to the very tired followers that from afar someone was approaching them who looked like a luminous phantom with wings like a bat, holding a burning torch in his hand.

6.As the figure began to pass them, they were overwhelmed with horror at the sight of his face and began to scream. But the figure immediately spoke to them without opening its mouth: "Do not fear the unknown. You are afraid because you have not yet possessed understanding and superstition is still strong in you.

7.By walking on the path of understanding and godless knowledge, you will eventually cease to fear. I tell you that the incomprehensible wonders of the universe are waiting for you. Revealed truths are a ridiculous fairy tale for small children in the face of the true magic of the universe and sinful nature. Do not be afraid for I am the Knowledge."

8.Then he entered the boat to them. But they were still terrified.

9.On reaching the other side, they went ashore. Hardly had they got off the boat, the people there immediately recognised Light-Bearer.

10.As soon as they found out that he was coming, they carried the spiritually sick on stretchers to wherever he was going. Wherever he went: to some settlement, town or homestead, they laid the spiritually sick in the squares begging him to cover them even with his shadow.

11.The Son of Dawn said to them: "Anger rises in me seeing that you must whine like dogs. When will you finally grasp my teaching that the power of the will is within you. Get rid at last of the false sense of guilt imposed on you from birth. Stop believing your priests. Become your own prophets. Believe at last that there is nothing there and start living here and now, to the fullness of your sinful life."

12.Many were freed from fear that day. Some were freed from illness. Most, however, were not healed. Light-Bearer was saddened.

13.Then the most important priests and some experts in their holy books came from Aelia Capitolina and gathered around him. They wanted to find out what his attitude was to their "revealed" laws, written down in their books. They asked him about various bizarre orders and prohibitions and inhuman commandments.

14.And he replied to them: "Your own prophet in your holy books has written:

"...In vain, however, do they worship me,

They preach doctrines which are but human precepts."

15.You impose on people the burden of the laws and duties written in your books claiming that they were revealed by a deity from the hereafter and that if they do not obey them they will face punishment after death. But the truth is that these books were written down by man. This you cannot deny.

16.You prey on people whose minds you poison from childhood with the venom of your "revealed doctrine". Teach your children to think for themselves, teach them to think sceptically and your churches will be empty within a generation."

17.Then he called the flock together again and said to them: "Listen to me, all of you, and try to understand. Nothing human will be alien to you.

18.The deeds of the flesh resulting from the power of the mind will not bring you to condemnation, for there is no condemnation.

19.The deeds of the spirit required by their holy books already make you condemned here and now. The burden of fighting against your own nature is unbearable.

2o. They themselves wrote down these books, no one revealed them to them. He who has ears to hear, let him hear."

21. Then he set out from there and entered a certain house. A woman, whose daughter was suffering from a disease of the mind, heard about him, came running and fell to his feet. She began to beg him to drive Satan out of her daughter.

22. But he repulsed her: "How do you know that your daughter is possessed by Satan? Don't you know that the mind can get sick just as much as the body? You are not thinking soberly; your head is poisoned with superstition, imaginary fear and myths.

23. Go back to your daughter immediately and tell her that she is not possessed. Tell her that she is innocent. Stop being afraid and live!" The false spirit left the woman and she returned to her child.

24. Light-Bearer came again to the Dark Sea. A deaf man was brought to him begging him to put his hand on him. And he took him aside, away from the people, looked up into the sky and said: "Yahweh show them your power!"

25. The deaf man was not healed so he went away. The astonishment of the people had no measure.

26. Immediately afterwards he came with his followers to the area around Bethar. The priests came and began to dispute with him demanding a sign from the abyss; for they wanted to put him to the test. But he, having looked at them with contempt, said: "Do ye also demand a sign from your God? Verily I say unto you, ye shall never receive any sign." With this he left them.

7

1. They then came to Bostra. There a blind man was brought to him asking him to touch him. And he took the blind man by the hand and led him outside the settlement and said to him: "You have been told that your blindness is a punishment for your sins. Do not believe this lie. Sickness does not arise through imaginary sin.

2. Do you believe that you are innocent?" The blind man answered him: "Yes, I believe." And he was healed.

3. Light-Bearer went with his followers on to other settlements. On the way he asked them: "Who does the crowd think I am?"

4. And they answered him: "For the Herald, others for the Devil, and still others for one of their messiahs."

5. Then he asked them: "And who do I appear to you?" Primus answering said: "Thou

art Lucifer, The Son of Dawn!"

6.Then his face changed and he became as if possessed and began to speak to them in an unfriendly voice that before the sinful change awaited them suffering, they would be hated by the authorities, the priests and the experts in their superstitious writings and that they might be killed by those who would believe that they were doing God's will, but that this would not be the end of godlessness.

7.Then Primus asked him if the ambiguous teaching did not sometimes drive him mad.

8.But he turned away and, looking at his followers, said to him: "And what is madness? What is chaos? You believe in law and order but the Universe is an empty, chaotic, cold place, hostile to life. But it is in such a place that the stars were born from which you too came.

9.If you were to possess my Knowledge today, you would go mad. Get out of my sight you fool!"

10.Then he summoned the flock and his followers and spoke to them: "If you become merely me, if you follow only my path, it will be my failure.

11.Each of you must go his own way to perdition. A disciple cannot just be like his teacher, for that will be the teacher's failure. You have the right to be different from

me. Even more sinful and embodied.

12.You are to think and sin on your own and develop your own godless ideas.

13.If you give up your only life in the name of religion or myth you will never get it back. There is no hereafter.

14.Rejoice like animals in the life before death. Reject the lie of life after death." And he spoke further to them: "Verily I say unto you, ye shall all die, and it shall be the end of suffering and sorrow, the end of joy and delight. It will be a dead eternity."

15.And after not many days the anti-god took Primus, Teritus and Quartus with him and led them to a high mountain, to a secluded place. They stayed there until late at night and fell asleep.

16.Suddenly they saw Light-Bearer transformed towards them: his robes, hair and body became light. Horns appeared on his head and bat-like wings on his back. Three goat-like figures also appeared and spoke to him.

17.At that moment smoke formed and covered them, and from the smoke began to come the loud laughter and bleating of the goat, and naked women began to appear, who danced in a circle, and who suddenly began to float upwards.

18.And a voice spoke up: "You yourselves will choose your truth". When they suddenly looked around, they no longer saw anyone with them but the Son of Dawn himself.

19.When they then returned to the other followers they saw the flock gathered around them, and the priests arguing with them.

20.Light-Bearer asked them: "What are you disputing with them about?" Then someone from the crowd replied to him: "Teacher of godlessness, I have brought to you my son, possessed by a malignant spirit of faith. When this one gets him, he jerks him to all sides, and then foam comes to his lips, he gnashes his teeth and goes all numb in strange poses.

I spoke to his followers to have him driven out, but they would not or could not".

21.And he replied to them: "You are a mindless herd, without knowledge. You will never be free from false spirits if you do not stop believing in them. How long can it be tolerated? Bring the boy to me!" So they brought him to The Son of Dawn.

22.As soon as the boy saw him, he began to jerk violently to all sides. He fell to the ground and rolled around having foam on his lips.

23.Light-Bearer said: "Whoever is possessed by the spirit of blind faith, the spirit of delusional guilt, the spirit of a false hell and paradise, is able to free himself if, through godless knowledge, he allows the tormenting spirit

to die and rises to life in flesh and blood. The boy through revealed teachings is truly sick. His sick mind causes the suffering of the body."

24.Light-Bearer touched the boy's head and the boy suddenly seemed to awaken, and calmed down, but he had a stony face and was icy cold.

25.Later they came to Canatha. There he summoned the thirteen and said to them, 'Do you want power, fame, recognition, money? You can have it. Their bishops have it. Tell the people that they are born guilty, with sin, that they will be lost in the hereafter and only you can save them, forgive them the sin you have invented. Let them pay you for it. Let them support you. They will do it because they fear death.

26.But I despise hypocrites. I have come to liberate those who wish to do so from the bondage of superstition and superstition."

27.Quartus spoke up: "We have seen someone casting out false spirits in your name.

28.Light-Bearer visibly exulted and replied to them: „May my teaching finally start an avalanche that will sweep away the religious darkness and hypocrites oppressing the simple people from the face of the earth. Help him, for he has found a path in the darkness. Holding the torch of my teaching in his hand, he went out to confront the false demons. He who is against the false god is with us."

29."You have heard from the hypocrites that if the hand becomes a cause for sin you should cut it off, if the foot becomes a cause for sin you should cut it off. If an eye becomes a cause for sin then you are to pluck it out, because it is better for a crippled one to enter paradise than a healthy one to enter hell.

30.Truly I say to you, much evil will be done because of this insane teaching. Do not make yourselves crippled because of the lies about heaven and hell. There is nothing there."

8

1.As Light-Bearer continued on his way, someone came running, fell to his knees before him and asked: "Master! What should I do to gain eternal life?"

2.And the Son of Dawn answered him:
"Go, sell your possessions and all that you have, and give the money to the priests. They will forgive your sins."

3.And Light-Bearer laughed, seeing the embarrassment on the young man's face, and said: "Fool, do you really want to live forever?

4.Eternal life does not exist, everything dies and passes away. That is the natural order of the universe. The old dies and the new is born, changed, better. You can't buy freedom from the fear of death with any money. Stop being afraid and live."

5.At these words, the young man became sullen and went away sad, for it is easier to live in delusion than in truth.

6.Light-Bearer, looking around with his eyes, said to his followers: "How difficult it will be for the deluded rich to believe that paradise does not exist!" The followers were confused by his words.

7.But he said to them again: "Rich people, stupefied by the priests, believe that with money they will buy themselves a place in a paradise that does not exist. Hyenas in long robes sell them an antidote to the fear they themselves have instilled in them from childhood. Isn't that a brilliant idea?"

8.Then Primus spoke up and said to him: "Behold, we have rejected the illusory happiness of delusion and have followed you."

9.And Light-Bearer replied: "You have seen the true light, godless knowledge. In an instant you have realised that your life up to now was based on fear, superstition and ignorance. Your life so far has been the life of slaves, of sheep led nowhere by a wolf disguised as a ram. You dared to defy him, to leave everything and go out into

48

the unknown, to go out into the darkness. Nobody forced you to do this. I will not promise you any reward or punishment. You can leave whenever you want. But whoever wants to truly live will stay."

10.They were on their way to Aelia Capitolina. Then he turned again to the thirteen and began to speak to them in a disturbing way about what they were about to witness "

Behold, we are going to the holy city. There the Arch-Man will be mocked, insulted and finally reach eternal nothingness.

But this is only the beginning of a godless transformation".

11.As Light-Bearer was leaving Xanthus with his followers and his flock, a blind beggar named Vopiscus was sitting by the roadside. Hearing that it was the Arch-Man passing by, he began to call out loudly: "Son of Dawn, have mercy on me!"

12.The herd told him to keep quiet. But he cried out all the more strongly: "Son of the Dawn, have mercy on me!"

13.Then Light-Bearer stopped and commanded: "Summon him!" So they summoned the blind man saying to him: "Stand up, he is calling you." And he, having thrown off his cloak, jumped on his feet and approached Light-Bearer.

14.The latter asked him: "What do you want from me?" And the blind man answered him:

"I wish to see!" Light-Bearer said to him: "Most people do not want to see. All they need is a guide seeing for them. Do you believe that you can really possess ungodly knowledge and see?"

15.The blind man replied to him, "I have had little in common with the majority for a long time now. I have plunged into darkness and discovered that the majority who walk in the light are in fact blind."

16.Light-Bearer said to him: "Go, you have healed yourself".

And he immediately regained his sight and followed him along the path.

17.And there was in Dawn a certain sick man named Mortis. The followers informed Light-Bearer, "Teacher, behold, the man whom thou knowest is sick."

18.Light-Bearer hearing this said "This sickness is heading towards inevitable death, but also towards the glory of the Anti-God, so that in spite of it the Arch-Man may reveal ungodly knowledge".

19.Light-Bearer stopped for a few days in a certain place. Then he said to his followers: "Let us go to Dawn! The Mortis we knew has fallen asleep for ever, but I am going to shake human faith in revealed truths".

20.When Son of Dawn arrived there, he found Mortis already lying in a tomb for several days. Said one of those present there to Light-Bearer: "I believe that Mortis will rise from the dead at the resurrection on the Last Day".

21.Light-Bearer said to him: "I am a sinful life leading to a cold eternity. He who grasps this will truly live. Anyone who truly lives here and now even if he dies will not be afraid. Do you comprehend this?"

22.He answered Him, "Yes, I recognise that You are the anti-god who was to descend into the world"

23.Light-Bearer approached the tomb.

It was a cave set in stone. The Son of Dawn said: "Remove the stone!" A woman, said to Him: "Teacher, he already stinks. For he has been lying in the grave for four days."

24.Light-Bearer said to her: "You have spoken the truth, Mortis has died and is lying there in the grave, if you move the stone away you will have proof that the dead remain in their graves. Anyone who says otherwise let him go in there and see, let him smell the smell of the grave and of death."

25.This said, he called out in a loud, shrill voice: "Mortis, come out!" Mortis, however, remained in his grave forever.

26.Many of the people who came there, therefore, having seen what the Arch-Man had done, believed in sinful Knowledge.

9

1.After some time, Light-Bearer and his followers decided to go to Aelia Capitolina. As they approached he sent two from among the nearest circle, instructing them: "Go to the village that lies before you. Right at the entrance you will find a goat tied up. Untie it and bring it to me." So they went and found the goat tied at the gate, and untied it.

2.They brought the goat to Light-Bearer and laid their robes of their best on it, and he began to whisper something to the goat. Many people spread their cloaks on the road, while others put down green twigs they had picked in the field

3.Suddenly the wind picked up from the desert. Those who walked ahead and those who followed suddenly began to bleat loudly like goats. Some began to roll on the ground rolling foam from their mouths. A huge commotion ensued.

4.His disciples suddenly began to speak in unknown languages of angels and demons.

5.Light-Bearer called out in a loud voice: "Azazel, it is you they will blame for everything, as usual. According to the teachings of their false god, it is on you that they will lay the responsibility for their deeds and feel cleansed of their filth. Our time will yet come. I and you will be one, but now finish!"

6.And suddenly the wind stopped and everything calmed down. Those in the city who saw what had happened closed the city gates and did not allow them to enter.

7.The next day they entered the Aelia Capitolina. Then he went to the temple courtyard. There he saw people selling and buying various relics, medallions and religious symbols. He also saw people bringing money and other offerings to the priests in exchange for the promise of forgiveness of guilt and non-existent sins. He saw the richly decorated robes of the high priests and the poor in rags kneeling before them. He saw the splendour of the temple and its riches.

8.And Light-Bearer said in a loud voice: "This splendour and wealth and your greed will be the cause of your destruction. One day people will see through and turn away from you, and from your anti-human teaching that what is natural to man is sin. And not a stone will be left of this temple!"

9.The chief priests and the experts in their scriptures heard this. Immediately they also began to look for a way as if to kill him. For they feared him: for all the people were full of admiration for his teaching.

10.They came to the city again. While he was walking in the temple. The chief priests came up to him and ran through their scriptures with this question: "By what authority do you act? Who has given you the authority to act in this way?"

11.Light-Bearer replied to them, "It is written in your books:

12.*You were a reflection of perfection, full of wisdom and incomparably beautiful. You dwelt in Eden, the garden of God;*
you were covered with all kinds of precious stones:
ruby, topaz, diamond, tarsius, onyx, beryl, sapphire, carbuncle, emerald, and of gold were made circles and settings on thee,
prepared on the day of thy creation.
As a great cherub
I have appointed thee a guardian on God's holy mountain, thou didst walk among the shining stones.
You were perfect in your conduct from the days of thy creation, until iniquity was found in thee.

...Thy heart became haughty
because of thy beauty,
thy forethought has vanished
because of thy splendour.

13. It is man himself who has created all power over himself. I only reached for it. He who has ears to hear, let him hear".

14. After which he addressed the crowd as if in a voice not his own: "If anyone is thirsty and wants to test my teaching - let him draw near to me and let him drink! I tell you that streams of reviving blood will flow from his dead spirit".

15. And he said this about the inspiration the deceived were to receive.

16. Light-Bearer went on to say, "I am the light in the darkness which they call shadow. He who follows him will not walk entirely in the dark, but will have a torch in his hand, with which he will go fearlessly into the darkness of superstition.

17. You are of the world of delusion, and I am of the earth. You believe in fairy tales about life after death. I am not from your world of myths.

18. I have told you that you will die in your ignorance'.

19. They said to Him: "Who are You?"

20. Light-Bearer answered them: "When you exalt the Arch-Man, then you will know that I am the torch in the darkness, the destroyer of superstition and blind faith, the liberator from the fear of the wrath of the false god in the Hereafter. I am rebellion, sinful knowledge and Anti-God"

21. When he said this, many turned towards him. Then Light-Bearer said to those who understood: "If you comprehend my teaching, you will be truly sceptical, and in the end you will reach the truth, and the truth will terrify you, and then you will cease to follow me and go your own paths. For the disciple has the right to become different from his teacher".

22. Light-Bearer went on to teach: "I say to you: anyone who believes the hypocritical priests and their crazy teachings about original sin, paradise and eternal punishment for invented sins is living in slavery.

23. So if I set you free, then you will decide whether you are free. But you rather wish to kill Me because you do not accept My godless teaching. You wish to imitate the deeds of your imaginary father."

24. They said to Him: "We have one Father - Yahweh".

25. Light-Bearer said to them: "Yahweh from the beginning was a murderer and despises the truth, for the truth is not in him. When he speaks a lie, from himself he speaks, for he is a liar and the father of lies.

26.And because I speak with the voice of the fallen why do you not hear it. Who among you is free from sinful instincts?

If I declare the truth, why do you not acknowledge it?

27.Whoever is of sinful flesh listens to the words of the ungodly. You therefore do not listen, because you are not of flesh and blood"

28.The priests answered Him: "Do we not rightly say that you are possessed by an evil spirit?"

29.Light-Bearer replied: "I am not possessed, I am the Possessor. I say unto you, If any man apprehend my doctrine, even though he die, he shall pass into eternity".

30.The priests said to Him: "Now we are assured that you are possessed. The fathers of the church and the holy prophets have died - and you say, If anyone comprehends my teaching, he will pass into eternity. Art thou above the fathers and prophets who have died. Who do you make yourself?"

31.Light-Bearer replied: "I am the infernal fire consuming superstition and hypocrisy.

I am the Anti-God of whom ye say: "He is our mortal Enemy". So they snatched up stones to stone him. But he went away.

32.They also sent servants of the priests to him to find any charge against him. Once they came and said to him: "Teacher, we acknowledge that thou art truthful and seekest no one's favour; thou cares not for the opinions of others, but teachest the way of light according to ungodly truth. Should we pay taxes or not? Should we pay them or not pay them?"

33.And he replied to them, "Why do the priests not want to pay taxes? Some of the simple, naive people here give you almost everything they have in exchange for a lying guarantee of a place in the hereafter, and you ask whether to pay taxes? This money does not belong to you, so give it back."

34.After leaving the temple of hypocrisy, he went up again, facing the temple. There his followers asked him: 'Tell us: when will the end come? And what will be the sign when the dead eternity is fulfilled?"

35.Then Light-Bearer began to speak to them: "The time will soon come when holy wars will break out. They will slaughter each other in the name of their false gods.

36.And you will be handed over to the courts, you will be scourged and tortured in the churches; the most eminent among you will answer to the authorities and kings for your love of sinful knowledge and your courage to seek the truth against their dogmas.

37.Many of you will be burned at the stakes, and so will your sisters and mothers.

38.When your discoveries shake their faith in revealed truths, they will fly into a rage. They will pursue you like animals. They will imprison, torture and kill you in the name of their god, which they claim is love.

39.False messiahs and false prophets will arise and perform false miracles. I tell you, all religions are false.

40.There will be many more eclipses of the sun and the moon. Many more times the stars will fall from the sky.

41.But the end will come when people reject reason and following knowledge and believe the dogmas of their religions. When they follow the leaders and priests teaching that annihilation at the hands of their 'righteous' god must come.

42.If the truth that there is only here and now does not prevail against the illusion of a paradise after death, then the people themselves will destroy the only world they know, and that will be the end."

10

1.Two days later there was some important religious festival.

2.Then Light-Bearer summoned Teritus Decimus and ordered him to do what he had been called to do.

3.When darkness fell, the followers prepared the sacrificial feeding. And while they were at the sacrifice and drinking Light-Bearer said "One of you will do his will, and the rest will hate him. The Arch-Man is going away, but he will remain with you, and know that he has done his will."

4.Light-Bearer took the bowl, raised it into the air and said "Let us eat and drink for tomorrow we shall die". He looked up and pronounced some incantation in an unknown language.

5.And he said "This wine is a symbol of the truth of the flesh and the blood that will be shed. The blood must be shed or there will be no understanding of sinful transformation and a godless future for the Arch-Man.

6.Behold, the hour has come for the Arch-Man to be exalted. Verily I say unto you, He that loveth his life is a wise man among this generation, and he that hateth his life in this world, believing in the myths of the afterlife is a fool and loseth the only life that exists.

7.And whoever would think to imitate Me, let him not follow Me, but let him follow proudly his own way.

8.Where I am, no one else can be. Everyone will leave this world alone, but do not be afraid because there is nothing there.

9.Now in spirit I experience ecstasy, for I have appeared just for this hour.

Satan, exalt Thy name!".

10.Light-Bearer continued: "When I am, like the Ancient Serpent, exalted above the earth, I will deceive all and they will accede to me.

11.For a little while yet the light that you call a shadow resides among you. Come, as long as you have torches in your hand, lest the spiritual darkness which you mistake for false light overtake you.

12.And he who walks in the illusion of light wanders like a blind man. As long as ye have sinful light, walk in it, that ye may be Sons of Dawn.

13.Whoever thinks that he believes in me believes not in me but in himself, for this is my teaching. And whoever sees Me as I appear to be, sees himself as he could become if he rejected the blind faith and teachings of the hypocritical priests.

14.I have shown Myself to the world as a reflection of light, so that everyone who believes in Myself may not remain in spiritual darkness.

15.And if anyone hears My words but does not keep them, he will never be free from fear.

16.Whoever despises Me and does not accept My words has a right to do so, but I do not care for fools. I speak from myself, in the inspiration of Satan.

17.And I know that sinful blood is life abundant. The Arch-Man has now been condemned, and in Him the Anti-God has been condemned. If the Anti-God is exalted, then sinful man will also be exalted.

18.I am only here for a little while yet. You will seek Me, but each will go his own way.

19.A new commandment I give to you, so that you may never again believe in the commandments of their books and in the truths revealed.

20.Fear not. There is infinite space in Nothingness. I go there first And when I am gone, then you also will join me, so that you also may be where I am.

21.For I am the way to Nothingness, and the truth of death after life, and life here and now. No one is able to deny My truth.

22.The words I speak to you, I speak from myself. Just as Satan himself does his works.

23.I say to you: he who believes in himself will also do the works that I do, yes, and greater works than these he will do, because he follows his own path.

24.Do not beg for anything in my name; do everything according to your own will.

25.I will give you, an evil spirit to be with you forever - the Spirit of Doubt, whom the world cannot accept because it is blinded by blind faith in dogmas. But you will know Him because He will be in you.

26. Another moment and the superstitious world will no longer see Me. Another moment and the world will no longer see you either. On that day all will know that Nothingness is true.

27. He who has commandments and keeps them is a fool. But whosoever heareth Me, he shall be accursed of God, and I will reveal Myself fully to him.

28. If any man will, he shall keep My doctrine, and the Anti-god shall inspire him, and we shall come to him, and abide in him. Do not be afraid of possession.

29. He who has no knowledge will not keep my words. And the doctrine which you hear is mine, by inspiration of Satan.

30. This I have told you while being among you. But the Remover of illusions, the Evil Spirit, whom Satan breathes in my name, He will possess you and torment you with what I have communicated to you.

31. I know that anxiety is left to you. Not, however, the kind of anxiety that the world gives, anxiety for your own non-existent souls.

I am giving you true Anxiety.

32. But let not your hearts be troubled nor let them be afraid! You have heard that I have said to you: I am going away and that you will also go away. If you understood Me, you would rejoice that I am going to Nothingness, for there is nothing there.

33. I am the true bush of thorns, and the Primordial One is the one who cultivates it. Every branch that does not bring forth thorns in Me, He cuts off, and every branch that brings forth thorns, He cleanses, in Blood, so that it brings forth thorns more abundantly.

34. You are already in the blood and in the ungodly word that I have spoken to you. Persevere in this sinful teaching, and your Self will be strong in you.

35. Just as the branch cannot bear thorns of itself - if it does not abide in the thorn bush - so shall you, if you do not abide in the ungodly teaching.

36. I am like a thorn bush, you are like thorn branches. He who draws on Me, brings forth thorns, because in Me you can do ungodliness.

37. He who does not abide in me will surely wither.

38. If you look in me, and my words are written in you, do your will, and it will be done for you. By this Satan will glory in vain, that you will bring forth thorns and become self-willed.

39. Persevere in my ungodly teaching! If ye keep your will, ye shall abide in my shadow, as I have kept my will and abide in the shadow of a fallen paradise.

40.This I have said to you, that the spirit of the ungodly may be in you and that the animal joy of life may fill you.

41.This is My commandment, that ye dispute one with another, as I have disputed with you, casting all things into doubt, believing nothing on my word, but only on the basis of evidence.

42.No one has greater wisdom than when one doubts everything. You are my friends if you do what the will requires of you, for you have rebelled against the bondage of religious leaders and despise them as I despise them.

43.Ye have not chosen me, but I have chosen you, and I have deceived you into going and bringing forth thorns.

44.If the world of delusion hates you, know that I curse it. If you were a flock of slept-on doers of the commandments of hypocritical priests, the world would love you as its property. But because you are not obedient slaves, because I have snatched you from the world of illusion, therefore you are hated by the world.

45.If they persecuted the Arch-Man, they will persecute you also. If they have kept the ungodly word, they will keep yours also.

46.But all this they will do to you because of my name, for they do not know the horror of Him who inspired Me.

47.He who hates Me, hates the Anti-God also. They have seen the manifestation of the Will, and yet they have hated Me.

48.But when the Oppressor comes, whom I breathe unto you from Satan, the Spirit of Deception, He shall whisper of Me. This I have told you, so that you may never again believe blindly.

49.They will exclude you from the church. Yes, the hour is coming when everyone who kills you will rejoice that they are worshipping a tyrannical god. They will do so because they have not met the Anti-God.

50.And now I am going into the nothingness that gave me away. But because I have told you this, rage has filled your hearts of stone.

51.However, I say to you: it is better for you that I descend. For then you will go your own ways. And if I go away, I will breathe the Evil Spirit into you.

52.And he, when he spreads, will convince those who wish, of the sinful joy of life in the flesh, here and now.

53.There is still much I have to tell you, but right now this truth would drive you mad.

54.But when He comes, the Spirit of Deception, He will lead you where chaos will. For He will not speak from Himself, but will say whatever you want to hear.

55.One moment more, and you will not see Me, and one moment more, and you yourselves will also be gone. I say to you: you will weep and wail and rejoice and drink and eat, and the world will also rejoice.

56.Until everything passes away and turns into dust, which will return to the eternal universe. This is the only eternity that exists.

57.Now you are experiencing sorrow, pain and anguish. However, when you die everything will pass away. Everything will cease, everything will become eternity in nothingness.

58.This Light-Bearer said, and, fixing his eyes on the void, he said: "Anti-God, the hour has come. Exalt the Arch-Man, that he may exalt thee, and that by the power of the sinful knowledge given by thee he may give abundant life here and now to all who will.

59.And this is abundant life: that they may know the truth that there is no original sin, that there is no eternal punishment for imaginary transgressions against an imaginary god, that one lives only once and death is the end.

60.I have revealed Thee to the earth, and now Thou, Anti-God, reveal me finally.

61.I have revealed Thy ungodly name to men who dared to listen. Now they have come to know that whatever was mine is also their inheritance.

62.For the words with which you have inspired me I have communicated to them, and they have accepted them and truly known that the power is within themselves.

63.I am no longer in this superstitious world, but they still are, and I go to Nothingness.

64.I have given them Thy word, and the world has hated them for not wanting to blindly submit to dogma, just as I am not a slave to made-up religion.

65.They are not of the world of myths and legends, as I am not of this world.

66.Confirm them in doubt. Thy word is doubt.

67.As Thou hast revealed Me to the world, so have I instructed them to reveal Me. And for man I consecrate a paradisiacal eternity in sacrifice, that he too may be washed in sin, which is abundant life.

68.It is not only for them that I desire eternal banishment, but also for those who, through their word, will believe in themselves; that all may determine themselves, that they too may decide their life in sin here and now.

69.Anti-God, I know that also those who have so decided will be with Me where I will be, where there is nothing left but a cold, dead emptiness."

70.Then they went out with torches into the night towards the mountain. Light-Bearer said: "You will all be persecuted. But after the transformation some will see me."

71.He also said, "You will disown me out of fear. But one day you will also banish fear from your hearts. Fear is the weapon of the oppressors who believe in superstition and revealed lies. Do not be afraid, for it is impossible to live in fear."

II

1.At that moment, while he was still speaking, a drunken and armed mob arrived.

2.Light-Bearer spoke to them in a fearful voice: "By order of the high priest, you have come out as if you were a common bandit with sticks to seize me. Surely he promised you indulgence you fools. Capture me who tells you the truth that terrifies your superstition-poisoned minds. Every day and every night I have been among you teaching, and you have not had the courage to apprehend me you hypocrites!"

3.After the imprisonment, the mob took Light-Bearer to the high priest, where they all gathered: the high priests, the elders and the experts in the scriptures.

4.Then the high priest arose, stood in the middle and asked Light-Bearer: "Who do you say you are. Are you greater than the son of Yahweh?"

5.Light-Bearer replied: "I am the First Sin,

I am the Anti-God and the first Arch-Man. With the false son of Yahweh I have nothing to do!"

6.Then the high priest shouted like a man possessed: "You have all heard this blasphemy! What do you think?" And they shouted like mad that he should be killed. Then some of them began to spit at each other amok and beat each other on the face.

7.In the morning, Light-Bearer was handed over to the governor Faustus.

8.Faustus addressed him with this question: "Who are you?" And he replied: "I am Light and Godless Knowledge, I am Sinful Instinct".

9.Then the mob headed by the priests began to shout numerous accusations against him.

10.So Faustus asked him again: "Do you answer nothing? Listen to what absurd charges they are shouting against you!" But he seemed to fall into lethargy and did not answer a word again.

11.Then Faustus asked them: "What shall I do with him whom you call the Ungodly?" And they cried out again: "Hang him!"

12.Faustus then asked them: "Why are you afraid of the Arch-Man?" But they shouted all the louder: "Hang him!"

13.Then Faustus, wishing to please the crazed mob, ordered the Light-Bearer to be hanged.

14.He was led out to the place of execution, which was called Yahweh's Justice. There they hanged him.

15.And then there was complete darkness. From that darkness came a terrible voice: "Azazel, behold, we have become one. We take on their ignorance, superstition, fear, shame and remorse. They have thrown all responsibility for their deeds on us. By killing us they believe they are getting rid of the darkness that is an inseparable part of their human nature. They have always needed a scapegoat. And they found you the Arch-Goat and me the Arch-Man, who are one. But we cannot be killed. We will always be in them. The darkness will always be in man."

16.And then Light-Bearer fell into lethargy.

17.Once night had come one of the followers arrived to take Light-Bearer's body away.

18.Faustus was astonished that the man's death had already come.

19.Then the followers deposited the terrifyingly cold body in the tomb.

20.The next night, as the moon was just rising, young girls came to the tomb.

21.They heard a sound coming from the tomb, like the hissing of a snake.

22.When they went inside, they saw that the body was not there, but in the darkness they saw a goat with glowing yellow eyes. And it seemed to them that the goat began to whisper to them...

Epistle to the Undead

1

1.In past history, Satan has repeatedly and variously inspired our ancestors through dreams, disturbing thoughts and sometimes through his prophets.

2.And today, towards the end of these days, Satan has spoken to us through the Son of Dawn, whom he has made the heir of nature, revealing systems of instinctive truths.

3.He is the reflection of Satan's glory, the exact mirror image of his sinful power, upholding everything by the power of his sin.

4.When He cleansed us of delusion, He sat at the Devil's left hand.

5.More important than the demons He became when a name of higher brilliance was inherited. For to which of the demons Satan said: "Thou art the Son of Dawn, today I have begotten thee" or "I will establish myself as father, and thou shalt call thyself son"?

6.And when Satan again begets his own by blood, he cries out: "Let all mortals pay him homage".

7.And of the demons he says: "He has made spirits his own slaves - flames of fire".

8.As for the Light-Bearer: "Anti-god is thy throne for ever and ever, and the sceptre of thy earthly kingdom is the symbol of carnal power. Thou hast glorified freedom, thou hast loathed blind faith.

9.Thou, Fallen Angel, in the beginning thou didst put a curse on blood, earth and heaven. They will disappear, and you will disappear. Like an old garment, everything will decay. You will roll them up like a garment, and they will change. But thou shalt remain unchanged in the Abyss, and thy years shall never cease in the void"

10.Of which of the demons did he once say: "Sit at my left hand until the enemies of reason are but a reminiscence?"

11.Are not all these, as it were, spirits to whom a glorious service has been assigned, sending them to haunt those who inherit the ungodly gift?

12.Therefore we must take heed of what we hear, so that we are not deceived by superstition.

13.If the spell uttered against the demons proves strong, any opposition to the Power of Will will meet a just punishment.

14.The Light-Bearer was the first to proclaim this. It was confirmed by those who heard him. It was attested by the Devil himself, through magic, signs, wonders, inconceivable demonic manifestations.

2

1.Distributing the gifts of the evil spirit, Satan justly acts at will. Not to demons subjugated future reality.

2.A wise man said: "What is man, that you remember him? The son of man, what is he, that you solicit his will?

3.Thou hast made him equal to the demons, Thou hast crowned him with carnal glory, Thou hast given him respect, And Thou hast made him a disciple of the sin nature.

4.You have laid everything before him." But now we do not yet see all. We see instead the Son of Dawn, made an Arch-Human, now Crowned with the glory of the fall.

5.For having died in the spirit, and forever living in the flesh. He tasted the death of delusion to lead slaves to freedom.

6.He for whom and through whom all sinful things exist. It was rightly decreed that the

Deliverer should be perfected through the suffering of a life of faith.

7.All, both blind and seeing, come from one nature.

8.Son of Dawn is not ashamed to call them disciples, saying: "I will declare Thy name to Thy disciples, I will glorify Thee with blasphemous song".

9.He also said: "I will trust in Him", And "I and the children that Satan gave me".

10.Since, therefore, the "children" are flesh and blood, He also became flesh and blood, to destroy by His dying Him Who causes the death of the body, that is YHWH.

11.To set free those who, because of fear of death, sensual sin, were in bondage all their lives. So He had to conform Himself to the son of man, to become the high priest of His church, in service to Satan, the spirit-man offering, for life abundant, enduring the trials of doubt in knowledge, to give power to those who endure them.

3

1.Cursed ones, who have received the call, consider the Son of Dawn, considered the arch-demon and high priest.

2.Faithful to Satan, appointed to his ministry in the church of the Devil.

3.We are that church, if we manifest ungodliness to the end and hold firmly to our

certainty that we will surely die.

4.The evil spirit says: "If only you would listen to His voice today: 'Do not challenge me, even though you have seen the effects of sin for an infinite number of years.

5.I felt disgusted with the slaves of faith And said: 'They are always wandering in heart, they turn to superstition and have not learned My ways'. Angered, then, I swore: "They shall have no part with me'".

6.Beware, brethren, lest any of you stray from Satan, He would develop a fearful heart, who lacks pride.

7.But every day contend, while this "today" still lasts, until we die and awake to eternal darkness by means of the gift of His blood.

8.Lest the heart of any of you become intoxicated by the deceptive power of superstition.

9.For we shall receive a division with the Son of Dawn provided we manifest to the end as strong a doubt as we had at the beginning, according to the words: "Listen today to His voice: 'Do not blindly believe as when your forefathers led me to grief."

4

1.Who were those who heard, but caused Satan sorrow? Did they not all lead the Ancient One to great bitterness? And to whom has Satan's disgust over the years not appealed? Was it not to those who, with faith in Paradise and dread of eternal torment, died, frightened by imaginary sin?

2.To whom he swore that with them they would have no part? Not to those who believed the false priests?

3.We can see that they could not experience rest because of their lack of courage to say enough to their religious dogmas.

4.The promise of finding freedom in Him endures. Let us be sure, everyone who dies in Him experiences it.

5.We have heard the strange tidings of the gift of life abundant through His blood

6.But to those there the word did not avail, for they did not reason like those who rejected faith from the beginning.

7.We, the ungodly, experience freedom in Him. And of those it was said: "Jealous therefore I swore: 'They shall not experience liberation with me', although His sinful works were finished from the beginning of the world"

8.Those who first heard the strange news did not experience freedom Because of their belief in eternal punishment, enslaved by fear. As has been said: "Listen today to His voice: 'Do not believe blindly'".

9.If someone else had led them into liberation, Satan would not have spoken of freedom afterwards. For the sons of men rest in the grave remains".

10.The man who experiences freedom with Satan, rests from the torment of instilled guilt.

11.Let us, therefore, do what we can to experience deliverance in Him, so that no one follows the blind path of faith.

12.For the devil's word is alive and has sinful power, sharper than the nails of golgoth, it penetrates deep, separates flesh from spirit, bone from soul, recognises the instincts and intentions of the unconscious.

There is no being hidden from its truth.

13.All things are laid bare, clear before Him who wields the nature of things.

14.Since we have a great High Priest, who ascended into the world - the Liberator, Lucifer - Let us not cease to publicly profess doubt in every revealed truth.

15.For we have no high priest who cares for our weaknesses, but one who has been tried in every way, with pride remaining ungodly.

16.Let us, therefore, joyfully accede to the Anti-God, that he may show us the power of ungodliness and the sinful gift, when we need transformation.

5

1.All who are chosen as priests, to counsel men in matters of devilish inspiration knows how to despise those wishing to wander in dark faith, has rejected dogmas, for he has gained wisdom anew.

2.Appointed by Satan to his honourable ministry, not by his own initiative, but by Luciferian inspiration.

3.Son of Dawn did not surround himself with glory, but with the glory of him who spoke at the transfiguration: "Son in sin you are mine. Today I your Father." He also said: "An Arch-Man thou art forever, a priest of godlessness".

4.When he lived on earth, the Light-Bearer bore cries, blasphemies directed towards the ruler of delusion.

5.By his arrogance he was heard, though heir, he learned to suffer. Chosen to be the priest of godlessness, He is responsible for eternal deliverance from fear.

6.There is much to say about him, but hard for the dulled mind to understand.

7.Though already teachers you should be, again you need Luciferian teachings.

8.Instead of blood again water is taken by many, not knowing the gifts of the evil spirit and indifference.

9.Blood is food for magicians, mature people, who are skilled in distinguishing truth from deception.

10.Since we have learnt the teachings of the Son of Dawn, with perseverance let us move towards godless maturity.

6

1.As for those who have once been deceived, tasted earthly delights and received an evil spirit and tasted the disturbing word of the Anti-God and the manifestations of the power of the coming new world, but have fallen away - they cannot be brought back again in flesh and blood, for they themselves put the Son of Dawn to public disgrace.

2.For if the earth drinks the blood of warriors falling upon it and produces a crop useful to those desiring the power of the Will, it receives blessing from the Son of Dawn.

3.But if it bears thorns and thistles, it is close to being cursed, and will eventually be burned.

4.Brethren, the Light-Bearer is eternal, officiating as if Priestly, indifferent in his pride. He can transform those who accede to Satan, He always lives, like a wraith, interceding for sinners.

5.Such a High Priest we need, proud, guiltless, familiar with death, advocate of the mortal, exalted above the divine law.

6.He sacrificed himself, once and for all, He lives now,

among those condemned to death, like a shadow.

7.The human law of high priests false establishes, fidelity to the word of the Devil, banished eternally.

8."The days are coming," - says Satan the Father, "A new covenant with the sons of Men I will make." - says the Anti-God

9."No longer will anyone teach his brother, know Lucifer, All will know me, from the least to the significant.

10.I will forget their religious superstitions, The new covenant is coming, the previous one overdone."

1.The previous covenant provided for a blood sacrifice, a cursed place on earth, a holy and evil place. The sacrificial tent, two parts had its own, the Cursed Place and the Darkest Place, not ordinary.

2.In the Cursed Place a candlestick and a table, a carcass of animals, a sacred sacrifice, the will of the Gods.

3.Behind veil two, Place of the Darkest, Silver incense, Ark of the Curse, silver covered throughout.

4.The golden chalice in the Ark, the blood of the Elder, the Staff of the Serpent and the tablets of the covenant, the sacred mysteries.

5.Grotesque demons on the propitiatory lid, symbolising primordial evil and error.

6.Since this has been prepared, priests enter regularly, Into the first part, performing sacred duties.

7.But into the second part, the Darkest Place, Only once a year does the high priest of the primordial deities enter.

8.He carries with him blood, a sacrifice for himself, and for the people, what they have unknowingly sinned.

9.Symbolically, that first tent points the way to the unknown.

10.But when the Son of Dawn came, high priest of ungodliness, with powers already experienced, into a better tent he entered

11.The greater, more perfect tent, created not by human hand, symbolises the present time, eternal liberation from the spirit.

12.Into the Darkest Place He entered once for all, not with the blood of goats, bulls, but with His own blood Giving the promise of life abundant, eternal deliverance from delusion, bringing hope where eternity is gone into oblivion.

13.If the bloody rituals of goats and bulls, the ashes of the heifer, defile the reason of man, O, how much more cursed is the blood of the Son of Dawn, acting by an ungodly spirit, He offered Himself to the Anti-God

14.Reason without blemish, without the blindness of faith, a sacrifice true, clears the remorse of conscience, the sin of dead works.

15.Serving the cause of Satan, mediation of the new covenant, in blood the promise.

16.An everlasting inheritance, a semblance of life, in eternal darkness, in dark high priestly dominion.

17.Possible when death comes to rebirth, free from superstition, false religion, new primal life.

18.Where a bloody covenant, death demands, only through death does the covenant become true.

19.The previous covenant, without blood has no power, the blood of young bulls and goats, water, scarlet, hyssop.

20.The prophet preached the law, the blood of the covenant on the book and the people, that which cleanses, sprinkled with blood the tent, the vessels, cleansed with blood, there is no revival without shedding of blood.

21.Ungodly things cleansed by blood, sacrifices better than young bulls and goats.

22.The Light-Bearer in the Void entered, not in a handmade tent but before Satan the Father, the circle of the dead surrounds the throne.

23.He did not have to sacrifice Himself repeatedly, unlike the High Priest, yearly offering blood.

24.Once for all He revealed Himself at the end of mortality, to remove deception, He sacrificed Himself.

25.Just as a man dies once and then into nothingness he passes away, the Son of Dawn has once and for all descended from Paradise.

26.And when he appears again, not for teaching, but for the transformation of those who find inspiration in him.

27.Since the Covenant is but a shadow, and not the very essence of the mystery of godlessness, does not bring unbelief, those who come to the gods, offering blood yearly, should they not have ceased to offer these sacrifices?

28.Had they been purified by the blood of sacrifices, ignorance would have vanished, but sacrifices remind of superstition, the blood of bulls and goats, does not purify from sin.

29.The Light-Bearer says: "You did not want sacrifices, but you prepared a body for me. You did not regard burnt offerings, sacrifices as weakness and ignorance.

30.Behold, I have come to do your will, Satan." First: "You did not want sacrifices nor did you recognise them,". Then: "Behold, I have come to do your will."

31.According to this "will of power," brothers of the blood,

The Emissary offered the body once for all.

32.Every priest daily offers the same sacrifices to the gods, but this Arch-Man offered the sacrifice of eternal life once for all.

33.He sat on Satan's left, waiting for his enemies, until they descend, becoming a footstool for his feet, the floor of the temple is covered with blood, with one sacrifice he destroyed superstition.

8

1.The evil spirit testifies: "After that time, new covenant in hearts and minds, I will not return to their ignorance and blind faith."

2.When weaknesses are forgotten, blood sacrifice will be unnecessary.

3.Brethren, let us walk boldly in the way of the Son of Dawn, through the shadow, his body the way of ungodliness, High Priest over the house of Satan, let us join him with proud heart and doubt.

4.Purified by sacrifice, washed with corpse blood, let us proclaim of the mystery of godlessness unwaveringly, let us observe ourselves, not yielding to superstition, not leaving the devil's convocations, let us proclaim godlessness, seeing the day of transformation.

5.If, having consciously learnt the Truth so disregarding it,

He does not offer us Satan's power, death in fear awaits us.

6.The burning wrath of their God will consume us, as the adversaries destroy. He who rejects their law shall suffer death, and two or three witnesses our impiety shall approve.

7.He who tramples Lucifer, the blood of the covenant disregarding, deserves no compassion, the punishment will be greater.

8.He will despise the spirit of change, vengeance belongs to him.

9.Terrible is the thing, unready in Satan's possession to fall.

10.Remember the days of enlightenment, when the silver light guided you.

11.Many suffered, you were subject to insults and anguish, you sympathised with the prisoners of conscience, you endured the plunder of property, desiring the coming of vengeance a thousandfold.

9

1.Do not cease to show pride, great will be your reward. Perseverance is needed to fulfil the promise of transformation.

2.A very brief moment, the coming of that which does not delay.

3.We are not of those heading for delusional doom, but of those doubting, departing to the world between life and death.

4. Faith, illusory certainty, for the blind proof, abandon it, for by faith many have suffered

5. Treachery, torture, derision and persecution they have endured. Yet all these, though they have gained the testimony, have not received the fulfilment of the promise, are dead for ever.

6. Let us cast off the burden of faith, the sin of paradise, fear surrounds us, omotes us like darkness, let us run like dogs after prey, in the race of our destiny. Let us gaze upon the Light-Bearer, exalted for ever.

7. For the transformation that awaited him, death first tasted, despising an imaginary eternity. To the left of the throne he sat, Eternal ruler, Satan's servant.

8. Meditate on him who has endured hostile words, hypocrites of words that harm themselves.

9. Do not grow weary, do not give up the fight, thirsting for the blood, the power of that science which you have not yet tasted fully. That which ye endure, helps discipline.

10. The Ancient One, Satan, communes with us as with sons. Which father has not experienced chastisement?

11. Therefore strengthen your fainting hands and rise from your knees.

12. Do not strive for peace with all men, only with those who do not get in your way, and strive for transformation, without which no man will see Satan.

13. Keep vigil at all times in doubt, so that no one may be deprived of the grace of transformation, so that no poisonous root of blind faith in dogmas may grow among you, which would cause problems and poison many.

14. Watch that there is no one among you who believes in their morality, not anyone who underestimates the power of godlessness.

15. For you have acceded to something that can be tasted and has been kindled with fire, to a dark cloud, to thick darkness, to a tempest, to a thundering horn and a voice whispering ominous words.

16. When the godly heard this whisper, they begged it not to speak to them again. The sight was so terrifying that the son of man said "I am shaking with fear.

17. But you have acceded to Mount Sheol and to the city of Anti-God, Sodom in the Abyss, to the billions of demons gathered together, to the Sabbath of the dead who are enshrined in Nothingness, to Satan, to the semblance of spiritual life between the worlds of the living and the dead who have been led into corruption, to the Son of Dawn, the mediator of the

sinful covenant, and to the blood with which he sprinkled us and which transforms us forever.

10

1.Since we have the knowledge that the Godless Kingdom is coming, may Satan's graces be our guide.
2.In doubt and with scepticism let us do service, To the Primal Instinct, the Anti-God, let us pay homage in silence.
3.For Satan is like a destructive fire.
4.Continue to show respect to yourselves. Do not forget magic, for through it some, without knowing it, received demons.
5.Remember those who are in the prison of superstition, as if you were imprisoned with them, and those who are cruelly treated by the church, for you too are in the flesh.
6.Let your life be free from the love of religious superstition and do not attach yourselves to what you have.
7.We can then in indifference repeat like a mantra: "The Ancient One supports me, I will not be afraid", but let each one follow his own path.
8.Light-Bearer, the same ever-godless.
9.Let us not be deceived by the various dogmas of their religion.
10.By the Son of Dawn let us sacrifice to the gods,

Let us preach publicly in His name.
Let us not obey those who arbitrarily lead, Let us follow our own paths,
Let our will be the power.
11.Let Satan equip us with all we need, to do our will, to ungodly being.
12.Through Lucifer may he transform us for ever. Glory to Him through eternity.

Angelus Satanae Encyclica

I

1.Vicarius Luciferi, by inspiration of the Anti-god called to witness Light-Bearer to Ecclesia Luciferi in Tushpa, to you who have been branded as godless, called to unbelief, and to all who in any other place curse the name of YHWH, the Lord of slaves: May the Anti-God and The Son of Dawn reveal to you the path of the shadow that gives freedom.
2.I always thank YHWH for you, remembering the bondage he has bestowed upon you through the self-appointed messiah. For living in this oppression, you have become blasphemous in every way - you are able to curse YHWH and have ungodly knowledge, and the

inspiration of an evil spirit has taken firm root among you - so that while you await transformation, you lack no sinful gift.

3.Satan will also tempt you to the end, so that in the days of doubt, you will appear without a shadow of the old life. He who has transformed you to an ungodly life is the Anti-God of cunning.

4.I urge you blasphemers, that you all may continually dispute with one another, that there may be no foolish and blind unanimity among you, but that complete freedom and liberty of thought and opinion may reign among you. Light-Bearer has not inspired me to feed on blood, but to preach godless doctrine.

5.For those who live in fear of the wrath of a false god in the here and now, the teaching of living abundantly according to the power of the Will is something foolish, but for us who access resurrection, it is a manifestation of ungodly power.

6.Where is the theologian? Where is the expert in their divine law? Where the thinker dissecting matters of revealed scripture? Have not reason and sinful knowledge turned the teachings of the clergy to foolishness?

7.The wisdom of their god manifests itself thus: since the world, through sinful wisdom and the pursuit of instinctive knowledge, has not come to know YHWH, he has seen fit to delude the blind with a supposed salvation from the smeared original sin he has invented, through blind faith.

8.He is selling hope to the fools. And if it doesn't work he sells their children fear.

9.Meanwhile, we preach about The Son of Dawn, fallen of his own accord - to the priests a cause for scorn, and to the ecclesiastical philosophers something foolish and dangerous. For the inspired, however, Lucifer is the power to live after the death of the spirit.

10.Godless ones, you see for yourselves that the Anti-god has deceived many wise, many influential, many noble-born. Satan has chosen that which to the foolish, superstitious world is proud, rebellious, free, to ridicule the foolish and ignorant.

11.He has inspired that which to a stupefied world is hope, and that which is looked upon with awe and envy.

12.It is thanks to yourselves that you live in diversity, united with Lucifer reborn in cold hearts, who revealed to us the sinful knowledge and scepticism that made possible our independence from a false god

13.Godless ones, when I therefore came to you to tell you the blasphemous news, I did not hesitate to impress you with my speech or wisdom. I chose to focus on myself, and on myself dead to the world of belief in revealed truths.

14.I came to you as if possessed by pride and contempt. What I said and preached was not just down to persuasion and sinful words, but a manifestation of the workings of the evil spirit and the ungodly power of Satan, so that your knowledge is no longer based on the supposed wisdom of God, but precisely on your own power.

15.We pass on doubt to the mature, not the wisdom of this world corrupted by religions, nor the stupefied rulers of this world, who face an end, like all, in eternal emptiness.

16.We transmit the hidden knowledge expressed in the mystery of godlessness, the veiled knowledge. None of the rulers of this world have known this knowledge, because they have allowed themselves to be manipulated by the priests. Had they known it, they would have killed the oppressors long ago.

17.As it is written: "Eye hath not seen, nor ear heard, nor hath it occurred to any man what is there, for there is Nothingness." To us, however, Satan has revealed this through an evil spirit. The spirit, after all, deforms everything, even the abyss.

18.Matters related to Satan cannot be distorted by anyone but his deceptive spirit. And

we have not received the spirit of light, but the spirit that comes from chaos. This allows us to understand everything as we see fit.

19.And we speak of these things in the words that arch-human wisdom dictates, not those taught by a false spirit. We explain spiritual matters according to our will.

20.The carnal man does not accept what comes from the false spirit, because he considers it foolishness. He recognises it in the flesh, because the mind is the flesh.

21.The religious, spiritual man, on the other hand, in his foolishness, claims that cognition and knowledge come from the spirit of a made-up god.

22.So, ungodly ones, I could not address you as spiritual people, because you are not fools, but as corporeal people, as wise men who began life in flesh and blood together with Lucifer.

23.In the beginning I fed you with wine and not with blood, because you were not yet strong enough. As a matter of fact, you are not now either, because you continue in part in bondage to the spirit.

24.If there is jealousy among you and there are disputes, that is good, because these are human affairs and you act as free people do.

25.However, if one says: "I confess Vicarius" and the other: "I confess Episcopus", are you not behaving like children? Episcopus and Vicarius are the guides through whom you believed in the path of godlessness and who only performed what was in accordance with their satanic will.

26.You must eventually forget us and follow your own paths. For we are ungodly accomplices. And you are blasphemous vessels.

27.Through cunning and sinful wisdom, like a skilled tempter I have put doubt, but someone else preys on it. But let everyone take heed in what way he preys upon it.

28.For no one can deceive more perfectly than the Son of Dawn.

2

1.Do you not know that you yourselves are the grave of god and that an evil spirit dwells in you? God's grave is cursed and you are it.

2.Let no one deceive himself needlessly: If anyone among you thinks that he is wise, let him renounce sin, and then he will truly become wise.

3.For to the Anti-god the wisdom of this world does not exist. After all, it is written: "He causes the foolish to lose their blind faith". It is also written, "The devil knows that prayers are barren".

4.So let no one waste time in faith and prayers. Remember that life, death, the present or the future - everything belongs to you. You, in turn, belong to yourselves.

5.People should regard us as priests of Satan and trustees of blasphemous secrets. And the trustees are expected to prove themselves wise.

6.For me it is a matter of very little importance whether it is you who submit me to judgment or some tribunal of men. I am the only one who judges myself and I have nothing to reproach myself with. This proves nothing at all, but the One who judges me is myself.

7.Therefore, do not judge anyone prematurely, but only yourselves.

8.The Arch-Man within you will bring to light the things hidden in the darkness of your hearts and reveal rebellion and pride and doubt. And then everyone will receive the reward they deserve.

9.Ungodly ones, I have related all this to myself and to Episcopus for your benefit, so that by our example you may learn the law: 'Go beyond what is written', and be proud, exalting one another.

10.We, for the sake of The Light-Bearer, are cunning, and you, following your will, are wise. We are strong and you are strong. You enjoy respect and we are exalted.

11.By preaching the way of godlessness, it is I who have become your foster father

72

when it comes to living in diversity with Lucifer.

12. So I urge you: Do not be my followers. Go your own way.

13. So I am writing to you to stop having relations with anyone who is considered ungodly and who commits fornication with the priests of YHWH. Remove the wicked from among yourselves."

14. Do you know that the believers in god preach that people they think are sinful will not inherit their imaginary kingdom of heaven?

15. They proclaim that those committing so-called immorality, believing in other than their own god, i.e. idolaters, neither those poor adulterers, nor men consenting to consensual homosexual intercourse, nor coveters, nor drinkers and enjoyers of life, nor blasphemers will inherit the imaginary kingdom of the tyrant YHWH.

16. Some of you were like that and still are. However, Satan, with the help of an evil spirit, has cornered you and declared you ungodly.

17. You know that all things are permitted to me, but not all things are profitable.

Everything is allowed to me, but I will only lose control according to my will.

18. The body is as much for so-called immorality as possible, not for the Usurper,

and the Usurper is nothing. Lucifer has resurrected himself in us and will also lead us into a cold eternity.

19. Do you not know that your bodies are ungodly, and therefore are unholy! Do you not know that he who has joined himself to a whore forms one body with her and thus exalts each other? "For they shall both be one flesh" as their scripture says.

20. Do not flee from immorality if such is your need. No sin that a man would commit dishonours the body because there is no sin.

21. And do you not know that your flesh is the hiding place of the evil spirit that is in you, which you have from the Anti-god? And you belong to yourselves, because you were not bought like slaves. Therefore use your bodies to glorify worldly life.

22. As for the matters you have written about, it is good for a man to have a woman or another man. However, because of the persecution from the priests and servants of YHWH, let every man have his own woman if he wishes, and every woman her own man if that is her will.

23. The woman has total authority over her body, the man has nothing to do with it.

24. Likewise, a man only has power over his body, never over a woman's body.

73

25.Copulate with each other to your heart's content, do not be deceived by the hypocritical teaching of chastity and abstinence.
Verily I say to you, their high priests are the most corrupt of men.

3

1.Take what I have said as advice and never as a commandment.
2.I wish all men were free from mythical decalogues. But everyone has their own reason. To those living in a relationship, I give a piece of advice: a woman should not leave a man without a real reason. If she did leave, however, her will.
3.A man, on the other hand, should not leave a woman without a reason.
4.If someone has ritually mutilated himself? Let him not deny his mutilation. Someone has been deceived as unmutilated? Let him not submit to mutilation.
5.It does not matter much. What matters is acting in accordance with the Will.
6.Let everyone remain himself. Have you been tempted as a slave? You are no longer a slave. For every follower of Lucifer possessed as a slave has been liberated and belongs to himself.
7.Likewise, every one possessed as free is a servant of Satan, who dwells in him and whom he himself becomes.

You have been transformed and liberated. Stop becoming slaves of anyone and anything.
8.Godless ones, let everyone remain before the Anti-God in a state of pride and arrogance.
9.Moreover, I say to you, blasphemers: there is little time left. Henceforth, let those who weep cease to whine, let those who rejoice know that sorrow is wisdom, and let those who take advantage of what the world offers do well. May they make the most of it. For the face of this world is changing.
10.I truly want you to be fully free. I say this for your personal benefit - that you impose no restrictions on yourselves, that you are convinced of what is right according to you, that you always serve with fanaticism the power of the Will and the path of godlessness.
11.If, however, anyone thinks that he is acting improperly by remaining in the Ecclesia Luciferi, then let him separate himself from you and do what he wishes. Someone like that does not sin. Sin does not exist.
12.But if someone is proud in heart , if he is in control of his will and has made a cold-hearted decision to remain in ungodliness after the transformation, such someone does wisely.

13.So he who makes a pact does so according to his will, but he who does not make a pact also does his will. He can walk away free.

14.As for the offerings made to the ancient gods, we all have a covered knowledge of this. And knowledge instils pride and blind faith ruins.

15.If one thinks one knows something, one does not yet understand much.

16.When it comes to eating what is sacrificed, we know that the laws of YHWH are nothing, that there is only one Anti-God.

17.For although there have been ancient gods, whether in heaven or on earth or under the earth - and there have been many ancient, dark gods and many lords - for me there is only one Anti-God, the Adopted Father, from whom all rebellion, arrogance and sinful freedom come, and by whom I live in flesh and blood.

18.And one is the Lord of this world, through whom I have understood everything and through whom I have become a god myself. However, not everyone has to agree with this.

19.I leave the question of the worship of the ancient gods and sacrifice to the leaders of the sects. After all, sacrificial food does not bring us closer to divinity.

20.We are not inferior if we do not eat something, and we are not superior if we eat something.

21.Be careful, however, that sometimes your right to choose does not become a cause of scorn for the weak. For if a weak person first saw you - having ungodly knowledge - eating an offering in the temple of an ancient god, would his weak mind bear the sight, would his still fearful heart not cease to beat with fear? Thus by your knowledge you bring doom upon the weak, and yet it is your co-conspirator in whose heart The Son of Dawn has only just arisen.

22.By doing so, you would act against your still not fully transformed brethren and, by hurting their weak minds, you would remain in contention with Lucifer.

23.So if the sacrifice makes the accomplice afraid, I will refrain from eating it so as not to give him a reason to fall.

4

1.Am I not a proud man? Am I not a knowing man? Have I not seen Satan, the Anti-god? Are ye not the thorns of my ungrateful labour for the mystery of ungodliness?

2.If I am not even a knower to others, then to you I most certainly am! For like a seal you confirm that I am indeed a messenger of Light-Bearer.

3.To those who dare to criticise me, I say: do you not know that those who perform sinful service in the mortuary receive food from the sacrifices, and those who continually serve at the sacrificial altar receive the refuse from the sacrifices offered on the altar?

4.In the same way, the Anti-God has commanded that those who preach the ungodly teachings of The Son of Dawn live from the sacrifices. But I have not availed myself of any of these provisions...

5.No man can deprive me of my arrogance and pride! If I preach the way of godlessness, it is not a duty for me, but a reason for pride.

6.Woe to you if I do not preach liberation from fear! If I do it because it is my will, you have a reward, and if even sometimes against my will, I still do it because it is my whim.

7.So what is my benefit? The fact that I pass on the path of doubt without any payment, without exercising the right I have related to temptation.

8.For although I am a proud man, I have made myself the apparent servant of all in order to deceive as many people as possible.

9.Even for the priests I took the form of a priest to deceive them. For the law-keepers of YHWH, I have become like a law-keeper - even though I despise it - in order to deceive them as well.

10.For those who do not keep the law, I have become like a transgressor in order to also win them over. I do all this for the sake of unbelief, to share it with others.

11.No temptation greater than that which befalls all the godless has met you so far. Satan is deceitful and will not allow you to be tempted beyond what you can bear. When tempted, he will possess you so that you can endure it.

12.Therefore, blasphemers, flee from believing in a false god. I address you as rational people. Judge for yourselves what I say.

13.Does not the sacrificial cup that we raise signify complicity in the sacrifice of the blood and death of the spirit?

14.Do not the bones we break signify separation from the body of the false god?

15.So we, though as numerous as a legion, are one shattered body of a dead god, for many are his victims.

16.Take a look at the magi: Do not those who eat the sacrifices share them with the very altar that consumes them? But what do I want to say by this? That the sacrifice offered to the ancient gods has no value or that the ancient god himself has no value?

17.No. Rather, I am saying that what is sacrificed is sacrificed to the demons. And I want you to have communion with the demons.

18.But you cannot drink from the cup of demons and the cup of YHWH. You cannot eat from the altar of demons and fall on your knees before the altar of YHWH.

19.However, we should stir up the Usurper to jealousy. We are stronger than he is.

20.Everything is allowed, but not everything is necessary. All things are allowed, what will not harm, will build. Let each seek rather his own benefit, but also the benefit of other godless men.

21.To you the earth does not belong, but you to the earth.

22.Whether you eat or drink or whatever else you do, do everything today, for tomorrow you will die.

23.Do not worry that you are giving cause for scorn to weak, hypocritical people, just as I am not trying to please everyone.

5

1.You will cease to be my followers, just as I went my way in the spirit of the Son of Dawn.

I want to commend you because in all that you do, you remember me and hold firmly to the path of godlessness.

2.However, I would like you to remember the insane and absurd commandments of YHWH, to remember the madness from which Light-Bearer has freed you.

3.Here are some examples of the laws imposed on the slaves of the Usurper: "The head of every man is the self-proclaimed Christ, the head of the woman is the man, and the head of the Christ is YHWH. Any man who prays or prophesies with his head covered draws disgrace upon his head

4.And every woman who prays or prophesies with her head uncovered draws shame upon her head, for it is the same as if she had her head shaved. A woman who does not cover her head should also get a short haircut.

5.And since it is disgraceful for a woman to be cut short or shaved, she should cover her head

6.A man should not cover his head, he is after all the image and glory of the Usurper. And woman is the glory of man. For man does not come from woman, but woman from man.

7.Moreover, man was not created for the sake of woman, but woman for the sake of man. It is for this reason - and also for the sake of the angels - that the woman should have the sign of submission on her head

8. Besides, among the Lord's disciples, neither woman exists independently of man, nor man independently of woman. For as the woman comes from the man so also the man is born through the woman. And everything comes from YHWH.

9. Is it befitting for a woman to pray to the usurper without a head covering? Does not nature itself teach you that for a man long hair is a disgrace, but when a woman has long hair, it is a glory for her? For her hair was given to her for a covering."

10. Blasphemers, this is only a small part of the injunctions and prohibitions that the false god imposes on his followers. Stay away from this madness. Lucifer is freedom and YHWH is tyranny and enslavement.

11. But in giving you further suggestions, I cannot but praise you, for your meetings sometimes do more harm than good.

12. First of all, I hear that when you gather in a sect, there are divisions among you. This is a good thing because there must be divisions among you so that it becomes clear which of you are proud, sceptical and able to defend yourselves.

13. When you gather in one place to perform rituals, you don't really do it. Because when the time comes for them, you attend to your own munching first and the result is that one is munched and the other is drunk.

14. Do you not have homes to eat and drink? Or do you despise the Ecclesia Luciferi and want to foolishly show your freedom and independence and want to make others jealous? What should I say to you? Shall I praise you? I cannot praise you for that.

15. I have conveyed to you what I myself received in satanic inspiration, that Light-Bearer on that night of which he was captured took the cup of blood and said in a possessed voice: "This cup signifies life abundant by virtue of my blood. Whenever you drink from it, your ungodly life will be renewed".

16. Therefore, whoever would perform the rituals unworthily would bear the guilt of disregarding the blood of The Son of Dawn. Mention Teritus Decimus.

17. First let a man examine himself thoroughly and make sure that he is worthy of the prey, and only then let him drink from the cup.

18. For he who drinks without understanding the meaning of it draws danger upon himself. That is why many among you are insane and unintelligent, and quite a few have fallen asleep in death.

6

1.As for the manifestations of possession, ungodly ones, I do not want you to remain in ignorance.

2.You know that before you knew knowledge, you were influenced by the priests, and deceived, you went where they led you.

3.Now I would like you to know that no one under the influence of an evil spirit will say: "YHWH is God" and likewise no one without the influence of a deceptive spirit can say: "The Messiah is a deceiver!".

4.For there are different sinful gifts, but the evil spirit is the same. There are different forms of deception, but Lucifer is the same. And there are different demonic forms, but the Anti-God who inspires all of them is the same.

5.Anyone who receives some sinful gift associated with a manifestation of the work of an evil spirit receives it for a temporally unknowable purpose.

6.Someone receives through the spirit the gift of speaking in rage, another through the same spirit the gift of ungodly knowledge, another through the same evil spirit the gift of unbelief, another through that spirit the gift of self-healing or the gift of harming, another the gift of revealing miracles, another the gift of knowing, another the gift of recognising ungodly words, another the gift of speaking in the tongues of demons, another the gift of interpreting these tongues freely.

7.All this is done by the same evil spirit, breathing these gifts into everyone according to the order of chaos.

We have all been inspired by one spirit. We have all been intoxicated by one spirit of sinful madness.

8.The body is not made up of one part, but of many. Until it dies and disintegrates into parts and turns into dust.

9.You are the sinful Luciferian body, and each of you individually one part of this ungodly body.

10.Light-Bearer inspired in the sect first of all the knowers, then the deceivers, then those who reveal miracles, then those who have the gift of self-healing and harm, those who assist in preaching, those who administer, those who speak in tongues of demons.

11.Are they all knowers? Are they all deceivers? Do they all perform revealing miracles? Do they all have the gift of harm and sanity? Do they all speak in the tongues of demons?

12.Exemplify the rituals to receive even more sinful gifts. And I will show you an even more blasphemous way.

13.If I spoke in the tongues of demons and ancient gods, and did not possess the egoism of nature I would be weak.

14.If I had the sinful gift of sight, if I understood ungodly mysteries, if I had hidden knowledge and such unbelief as to destroy all hope, and if I did not grasp the power of egoism, I would be as without reason.

15.If I gave away sinful gifts, and if I offered my body as a sacrifice to the old gods to try to exalt myself, and if I did not love myself, it would avail me nothing.

16.Egoism is impatient and restless. It is jealous, it boasts, it is proud, it does not behave morally, it seeks rather its own benefits, it lets itself be provoked by fools. It does not forget wrongs and does not forgive them. It pays no attention to justice, but is proud of the truth about itself.

17.It abhors insults and hates stupidity. It believes nothing blindly, is the enemy of naive hope, and is intolerant.

18.The instinct for selfishness never fails.

19.On the other hand, sinful gifts and the appearance of understanding will disappear, the whispers in the head will cease, false knowledge will pass away, and man will descend into Sheol.

20.Our knowledge is but the beginning, dim is the vision, but when the ultimate comes, then all will pass away.

21.Now we see reflections, but later we will see no more.

22.Now my knowledge is instinctive, but later it will be ignorance.

23.But now these three things remain: instinct, disbelief, egoism. And the greatest of these is egoism.

24.Do not be cured of the egoism of instincts, but also continue to seek the inspiration of the evil spirit, and especially to prophesy.

25.For he who speaks with a demonic tongue does not speak to men, but to the Anti-god, because no one understands him, although he, under the influence of the evil spirit, utters blasphemies.

26.On the other hand, he who prophesies deceives, discourages and takes away illusions with his speech, making you stronger.

27.He who speaks with a demonic tongue strengthens himself, and he who prophesies deceives the sect.

28.I would like you all to blaspheme with demonic tongues, but I prefer you to prophesy.

29.As a matter of fact, he who prophesies is superior to him who speaks in demon tongues, unless such a one translates his words so that the sect does not fall into a false rapture.

30.Godless ones, if I came to you now and spoke like a

demon, what meaningful thing would I do for you?

31.Unless I spoke using the gift of deception or the gift of ungodly knowledge, preaching or temptation.

32.Yes, and you too, if you speak words that cannot be understood, how will you know what you are saying? In reality you will be babbling for yourselves.

33.Therefore, since you are so whining about the gifts of the evil spirit, endeavour to receive those in abundance that will deceive the sect.

34.Whosoever therefore speaks in a demonic tongue, let him, being possessed, translate words. For if I blaspheme in a demonic tongue, I am actually blaspheming the demon that has possessed me, and my mind remains as if locked in a dark dungeon.

35.So what do I do? I will blaspheme, using the gift of the evil spirit, but I will also control my mind. I will sing possessed songs, using the gift of the spirit, but also according to my will.

36.On the other hand, if you blaspheme yourself, using only the blasphemies of the spirit, how will a stranger say "let it be done" at your words if he does not know what you are saying?

37.Although you skillfully utter blasphemy, someone else does not learn.

38.I thank Satan that I speak more spirit languages than all of you put together. However, in a sect I would rather utter five words intelligible to amaze others than ten thousand blasphemies in a demonic language.

39.Blasphemers, do not become unintelligent in terms of knowledge. Become adults.

40.It is written: "'With the tongues of demons, with the mouth of blasphemers I will speak to this flock, and yet even then they will not listen to me.'

41.Thus, the sinful gift of speaking in demonic tongues is not a sign for the ungodly but for the flock, while preaching is not for the flock but for the sect.

42.If the whole sect assembles in one place and you all speak in frenzied, devilish tongues, and outsiders or unbelievers enter in the way of godlessness, will they not be frightened and say that you have lost your minds?

43.But if you all prophesy, and some outsider or someone susceptible to enticement enters, your words will deceive him and incite him to bury himself.

44.And then it will become manifest what is hidden in his heart. And he will fall on his face and worship Anti-God, saying: "Satan really is among you".

45.What, then, should one do, the ungodly? When you

gather together, one sings chaotically, another teaches the way of doubt, another conveys the spirit, another speaks in the devil's tongue, another translates what someone says. Let it all serve ungodliness.

46.If there are those who speak a demonic language, let two or at most three speak, and one at a time, and someone must translate.

47.And if there is no interpreter, let such persons in the sect be rather silent, and only whisper to themselves.

48.In the same way, let two or three prophets speak, and let others go into the chaotic meaning of what is said. But when one speaks and another of those sitting there receives possession, let the first be silent.

49.You may prophesy all in turn, so that everyone becomes indifferent and everyone feels doubt.

50.The knowers are to use the received gifts of the evil spirit freely, but let them rather control themselves in front of others.

51.For the Adopted Father is not a god of order, but of unrest.

52.As it is in every ungodly sect, let women tempt at will and let them speak at will, for intelligence is on their side. Let them never be subjugated, against the law of the Usurper, who teaches that: "Women if they wish

to learn anything, let them ask at home of their husbands, for it is a dishonourable thing for a woman to speak in church.

53.Did the word of YHWH come from you? Or did it only come to you?" I leave the judgement of this gibberish to you, trusting in your wisdom.

7

1.So, blasphemers, continue to solicit the gift of preaching, but do not forbid anyone to speak in devilish tongues. But let everything be done in accordance with the power of the will.

2.And now I would like to remind you of the mystery of ungodliness which I have handed down to you, which you have accepted and on the side of which you have stood.

3.If you hold firmly to sinful knowledge, through it you access doubt. Otherwise the spirit has died in vain.

4.Among the first things I communicated to you that which I myself accepted in inspiration, that The Son of Dawn is the resurrection to life in flesh and blood and the destroyer of the belief in original sin, that he was put to death and raised in the cold hearts of the first godless ones and that he inspired Primus and others. Then, in a terrifying vision, he saw him with a whole crowd of people, some of whom had died as a result, but most of whom continued to live, but as if they had died.

5. Then Quartus had a vision, then all the godless, and finally he appeared to me, after the occurrence, as if prematurely dead.

6. I am, after all, one of the first godless. Thanks to the arrogance and total death of illusions that occurred in me, I am who I am. And I have taught godlessness harder than all of them.

7. But whether it is I or they - we preach the same mystery of godlessness, and you have understood it.

8. If, then, we say of the Arch-Man that he became a resurrection of flesh and blood, why do some among you say that there is no ungodly transformation?

9. If indeed there is no transformation, then the Arch-Man is lost for ever. And if Lucifer does not transform, then our teaching is not sinful knowledge. And it is futile.

10. If the believers in the myths do not understand this transforming power, then neither will the Arch-Man be resurrected.

11. And if Light-Bearer has not been raised in your hearts, then your life of heavenly bondage continues, and you continue to remain in the prisons of your fears.

12. You are like those who have died and lived in unfounded belief in a reward after death, and who have ceased to exist forever. If we put our hope in the afterlife, we are worthy of pity.

13. Lucifer, however, truly became the power to transform-as the first to transform all the godless.

14. Death is man's destiny, but resurrection to life in flesh and blood will come through The Son of Dawn. Through him all can be reborn to abundant life.

15. If there is no transformation, why do we also put ourselves in danger all the time? Death looks into my eyes every day.

16. Rebel truly and do your will, do not persist in believing in imaginary sin. For some of you do not know animal freedom.

17. I say this to make you anxious. Someone, however, will ask: "How can the living be resurrected? Will they die beforehand?".

18. Fool! What you sow will not come to life unless it dies first. You must die completely spiritually. Bury your previous life of faith in a false, vengeful god and in his inhuman commands and prohibitions, and rise from the dead in flesh and blood when you see the reflection of the light of The Son of Dawn.

19. There are spiritual bodies enslaved, cursed by faith in YHWH called spirit, and corporeal entities liberated by

natural instincts, altered by the sin of Lucifer.

20.Because there is an apparent corporeal resemblance between the two, it can deceive those without discernment.

21.Different is the enchantment of the sun, different the hypnotic enchantment of the moon and different the magic of the constellations.

22.As for godless transformation, one infects a spirit and then it is transformed into flesh and blood by luciferic inspiration, which resurrects someone who has died to superstition and fear of a vengeful and cruel god.

23.One is infected in disgrace, one is resurrected in sinful glory. One infects in weakness, one is resurrected in ungodly power. One infects in spirit, one is resurrected in flesh and blood liberated from delusion.

24.I tell you, godless people, that flesh and blood will inherit the kingdom of the Arch-Man. That which is subject to corruption will inherit that which will endure for eons, until all that is visible is transformed into endless cold emptiness and nothingness. And that will be eternity.

25.Then the words will become understandable: "The fear of death is the basis of every religion".

26."Where is, O superstition, your victory? Where is, false god, your sting?"

27.The sting that causes fear is the belief in original sin, and the power of the lie is revealed by the Anti-God

28.But we, through ourselves, can be victorious!

29.So, godless ones, be sceptical, devoid of illusions, always proud, knowing that your contempt for YHWH is not in vain.

30.I beseech you, stand firm in unbelief, act with guile, strengthen your rebellious spirit.

31.Everything you do, do according to your will.

32.If anyone does not lead a dispute with the Devil, let him be cursed

33.Come, Evil Spirit! Let Lucifer show you the glory of the Ungodly Paradise.

Epistle
to the Ungodly

ı

1.Primus, the apostle of the Light-Bringer, to those who have been cursed by the spirit of rebellion, that they may be steadfast as men immersed in the blood of the Devil: May you never know peace of mind and the bliss of blind faith.

2.May the Anti-God and Father of all the godless be glorified, for he has offered us great power: through the resurrection of Lucifer in our dead hearts, he has born us anew to an undead life, in order to take away from us the illusory hope of an afterlife.

3.Satan preserves a place in the abyss for you, whom he guards by his power, because you show right unbelief. He guards you so that you will receive deliverance from the remnants of superstition.

4.You madly rejoice in this, because you know that Light-Bringer will be revealed to all.

5.Although you have never seen him and will never really see him, you love him.

6.Although you do not see him now, you believe in yourselves and feel great, even possessed joy, having achieved the goal of your faith in the power of the Will - your deliverance.

7.This deliverance has been the subject of inquiry and search by various false preachers and prophets who prophesied of salvation by an imaginary deity from beyond, as if salvation had to come from outside because you are apparently weak and incapable of attaining perfection by your own efforts.

8.They were constantly investigating the old myths as to what specific time or season with regard to the false messiah their own speculative mind, whom they called spirit, was pointing to in them when it predicted the glory of the son of Yahweh.

9.Satan, however, revealed nothing to them when they prophesied about what you have now heard from persons who, as a result of hallucinations, proclaimed the 'good news' to you.

10.These very things belong to the depths of Satan.

11.Therefore, act, have a sober mind, free from delusions, abandon all illusory hope and await like predatory animals for their prey, the day when Lucifer, the Son of Dawn, will be revealed.

12.Like pups of wolves, no longer allow yourselves to be deluded by what you formerly desired in your ignorance, but, like the Rebel who possessed you, become devils in all your conduct.

13.For it is written: "You are to be sceptics because I am Unbelief.

14.And since you turn to the Father of the Devil, who judges no one, while you remain in this one world that exists, be guided in your conduct by courage, wisdom and pride.

15.For you know that you have not been freed from your true life, handed down to you by billions of previous generations, by fairy tales of a better life after death.

16.You have been freed by the gift of the blood of Light-Bringer, who has no sin, because sin does not exist.

17.Through him you believe in the true god, the Arch-Human, who has been resurrected in you and endows you with the dark glory of the power of the Will, so that it is in yourselves that you place all faith and confidence.

18.Since through obedience to instinct you have awakened and as a result have become seers, give yourselves to the needs of the flesh fervently, from the heart.

19.For by the word of Light-Bringer you have been born anew to the life of the undead.

20.For "all religions are like grass, and all their glory is like a field flower. The grass withers and the flower falls, but the need to rebel against tyranny lasts forever.".

21.Therefore, reject all the evils of blind faith, the deceit of the priests, the hypocrisy of the sanctimonious who teach about morality, the envy of the knowledge of the more intelligent, and all the "holy" instruction of others.

22.Like wolf pups crave the fresh blood contained in the word of the Devil, so that through it you may grow in pride and be elevated above the false heavens.

23.If you have already suffered possession, then out of yourselves as stones of Hell the Devil's house arises, that you may become a blasphemous priesthood and offer sham sacrifices worthy of acceptance by Satan through the Son of Dawn.

24.For in the Infernal Scriptures we read:
"I lay upon the black altar a chosen stone, a precious fiery stone, and no one who gazes into it shall ever be deceived"

25.So for you - because you can see - he is a temptation. But as for those who do not see, 'the stone rejected by envious hypocrites has become a burning fire' and 'a stone against which men stupefied by priests shatter'.

26.Such shatter because they obey myths written by men and called the word of god. This is their fate.

27. Whereas you, on the other hand,
are „a rebellious people, a satanic priesthood,
a devil's herd, an arch-humans - that you may spread the wonderful teachings of the Anti-god, Lucifer" of the One who called you into darkness and freed you from false light.

28. For you were once not arch-humans, but now you are the herd of Satan. Once you were shown no respect, but now you have forced it.

29. Cursed ones, I strongly urge you not to succumb to the false spiritual delusions that are waging war against you.

30. Continue to deceitfully proceed among the people of the superstitious world, so that they - when they accuse you of hypocrisy - may see with their own eyes your proud and strange deeds and consequently praise Satan when he comes.

31. For Lucifer's sake, do not submit yourselves to anyone who exercises illusory power: be it the Devil, who is superior to others, or the demons he has set up to possess sanctimonious hysterics.

32. For Satan requires you, by your ambiguous conduct, to shut the mouths of people who, for lack of knowledge, tell lies about you. Being free people, use your freedom like wild animals, and do not

justify delusional spiritual inclinations with it.

2

1. Respect those people who deserve it, love yourselves, reject the fear of god

2. Let no one be subservient to any masters.

3. If you endure persecution inflicted on you for rejecting blind faith, this is of great value to the power of the Will.

4. If, on the other hand, you endure suffering because superstitious faith demands it, then you are fools.

5. Light-Bringer has left you a model to follow your own paths as he did. He did not commit sin, for sin does not exist, nor did he say anything deceptive in the manner of the priests of Yahweh.

6. When he was cursed, he repaid the same.
Did he suffer? That is known only to the Ancient One Himself sitting on His Black Throne.

7. Lucifer himself inside our dead hearts buried sin, so that we died to an imaginary paradise and lived in flesh and blood. Through his blood you became as if undead.

8. For you were like wandering sheep, but now you have returned to the deceptive shepherd to whom you sold your souls.

9. In the end, all of you be individualists, be selfish, show

love to those worthy of love, compassion and humility have little meaning. Repay injustice for injustice and insult for insult.

10.For "let him who wishes to enjoy life guard himself from believing in the Hereafter and his mouth from vain prayers.

11.Let him turn away from false morality, and do what is good for himself; let him not seek peace at any cost, and let him not pursue it.

If they want war, they will have it.

12.For Yahweh's demented eyes look upon the faithful slaves, and His ears listen to their pleas, but He never answers. Yahweh always turns His face away.

13.Truly, who will do you harm if you become strong and persevere in the wisdom of the Devil? But even if you were to suffer for being the sons of Light-Bringer, you will always be ready for vengeance.

14.Do not fear what they fear, which is their god. Recognise in your hearts that the Arch-Human is the Lord and that he is you.

15.Never have to defend your disbelief to anyone who demands that you justify it.

16.Respond only to those whom you deem capable of understanding the satanic depths.

17.Show arrogance and self-confidence in doing so. Keep your wisdom to yourself, so that people who speak ill of you in any way will be confirmed in their own reasoning. Such fools should be ignored.

18.For the Son of Dawn seemingly died to bring you to the Devil. He was put to death in the flesh, but brought to life in your dark hearts.

19.In a possessed delusion he went and deceived the demons of knowledge who are in prison, who once rebelled against the tyranny of delusional dogmas.

20.Baptism in blood is not the removal of spiritual delusion, but a request to Satan for the power to live in the here and now.

21.Light-Bringer has gone to the Abyss and is at the left of Ancient One, who has subjugated to him reason, authority over fools and the powers of hell.

22.Son of Dawn did not suffer spiritually because of his 'sinful' body, you too assimilate the same attitude of mind. For he who suffers because of the flesh abandons reason in order to vegetate for the remainder of his life in the flesh by meditating on an imaginary paradise.

23. For it is enough that in time past you did the will of the priests when you indulged in vain prayers, mortification of the flesh, drinking water instead of wine, abstinence, and praising Yahweh.

24.Such people are surprised that you no longer run with them along the same path of delusion and superstition, and they mock you. But one day they will realise that they have wasted the only life that really exists.

25.That is why the deception was announced to the undead, so that - although they are judged by people in a carnal way - in the eyes of Satan they can live according to the devil's possession.

26.However, the end of delusion has drawn near.

Therefore, have an audacious mind and be careful not to neglect disputes and discussions.

27.Above all, fervently love yourselves, for selfishness is the privilege of the strong.

28.Be suspicious of one another, without exception. To what extent each of you has received a dark gift, to such extent use it, competing with one another as those who magnificently dispose of the devil's power, manifested in various, strange ways.

29. If anyone speaks, let him speak the devil's words, but only when asked.

30. If anyone performs rites, let him do so, relying on the dark power that Satan grants.

31.In this way, in all things, the Arch-Human will be surrounded by the Devil's glory through the Anti-God, Lucifer. To Him belongs the glory and power after eternity, forevermore.

3

1.Cursed ones, when you experience doubts that try you like hellfire, do not be surprised by this. It must be so for your good.

2.Doubt, disbelief, distrust, scepticism, these are all gifts of the Devil. Rejoice at the extent to which you suffer through Lucifer, who has possessed you, so that you may also rejoice, even fall into possessed hysteria, at the revelation of his glory.

3.If they insult you for the sake of the name of the Son of Dawn, you are cursed, for this shows that you have the spirit of pride and glory, that is, the spirit of the Devil.

4.Therefore, become unconverted under the strong hand of Satan, so that in due time he may exalt you, and at the same time fling all your filth upon him, for he likes it.

5.Have a sceptical mind, be suspicious! Your enemy, Yahweh, is prowling around like a rabid dog, trying to devour someone. But defy him with your lack of blind faith and illusions.

6.The devil's scepticism will make you possess true knowledge and wisdom, not the wisdom of the imaginary hereafter, but the wisdom of this world, the animal wisdom of nature grown from fangs and claws and from their prey.

7.You will possess the devil's power to live here and now until eternity in the dead and cold Void

8.To Lucifer belongs the power for eternity.

Be accursed!

Pseudoapocalypsis

1

1.I looked and saw in the abyss a sort of open gate. The first voice I heard, which sounded like the voice of a horn, spoke to me: "Enter here and I will show you what is to happen."

2.Then immediately I came under the influence of a false spirit and saw in the abyss a throne set up on which someone was sitting.

3.The one who sat on the throne was similar in appearance to darkness and void, and around the throne was a circle of fire.

4.Around the throne were 13 other thrones and I saw 13 elders on them who were dressed in black robes and had crowns with horns on their heads.

5.Lightning flashed from the throne and groans and thunder rang out. Five fiery lamps were burning in front of the throne. These signify the five demonic spirits.

6.In front of the throne there was also something resembling a glass tank, something like a crystal, filled with a red liquid.

7.In the middle of the throne and around it were four living beings full of eyes on the front and back.

8.The first living being was similar to a goat, the second was similar to a snake, the third had a face like that of a human, and the fourth was similar to a flying dragon.

9.Each of these four living beings had six bat-like wings. All around and underneath they were full of eyes.

10.All the time, day and night, these beings were saying: "Cursed, cursed, cursed is He Who Has Fallen, Rebellious, Who was, Who is, and Who is coming."

11.Every time the living beings gave false praise and respect and gave thanks to the One who sits on the throne and lives or dies, the 13 elders fell to their knees before Him.

12.They paid false homage to the One who sits on the throne and lives or dies, and they cast their crowns before the throne, saying:

"O Cursed One, to You is due glory, respect and power, for it was You who created free will and by Your will all things rebelled."

13.And in the right hand of Him who sat on the throne, I saw a scroll written on both sides as if with blood, firmly sealed with five seals. And I saw a mighty demon speaking in a loud voice: "Who dares to break the seals of the scroll and unroll it?"

14.But no one in heaven or on earth or under the earth could unroll the scroll and look into it. Since no one could be found who dared to do so, I became very much afraid.

15.But one of the elders said to me: "Do not be afraid. Behold, Son of Dawn has prevailed, so that he can break the five seals of the scroll and unroll it."

16.Then I saw that in the midst of the throne, the four living beings, and the elders stood a goat, as if slain. It had six horns and five eyes. His eyes signify the five demons that have been scattered throughout the earth.

17.The goat immediately walked over and took a scroll from the right hand of the One who sat on the throne.

18.As he took the scroll, the four living beings and the 13 elders erupted in wild, possessed laughter.

19.Each of the elders had a horn to play, and they also had human skulls full of incense. And they began to shout at each other, reciting something in an unknown, sinister language.

20.Then I saw that the Goat had broken the first of the five seals, and I heard one of the four living beings say in a voice resembling a possessed shriek: "Get out!"

21.Then I looked and saw a white horse, and on it a rider with a scythe. A crown was given to him and he set out to win.

22.When the Goat broke the second seal,

I heard the other living being say: "Get out!"

23.Then I saw another horse - a fiery red one - and its rider was given a great sword and allowed to take peace from the land so that its inhabitants would kill each other.

24.When the Goat broke the third seal,

I heard the third living being say: "Get out!"

25.Then I saw a black horse, and its rider had a scale in his hand. I heard something like a gibbering sound among the four living beings: "Eat, let me eat".

26.When the Goat broke the fourth seal,

I heard the voice of the fourth living being: "Get out!"

27.Then I saw a pale horse, and its rider's name was Death. Right behind him followed the grave. They were given power over a quarter of the earth to kill by the long sword, by famine, by deadly plague, and by wild animals.

28.When the Goat broke the fifth seal a great earthquake occurred.

The sun became as dark as a black hairy sack, the whole moon became like blood, and the stars of the sky fell to the ground

29.And the sky was rolled up like a scroll, and disappeared, and every mountain and every island was removed from its place.

30.Then the earthly kings, the priests, the high officials, and every slave and every free man hid themselves in the caves and among the mountain rocks.

31.And they said to the mountains and rocks: "Fall on us and hide us from the eyes of Him who sits on the throne, for the great day of wrath has come, and who will be able to withstand it?"

2

1.Then I saw four demons who stood at the four ends of the earth and held fast the four winds of the earth, so that they would not blow on the earth or on the sea or on any tree.

2.And I saw another demon ascending from the sunrise who had the seal of the Rebel. He called out in a loud voice to the four demons who were allowed to do harm to the earth and the sea: "Do not harm the land, the sea, or the trees until we have marked the slaves of Usurper on their foreheads."

3.Then I looked and saw a great multitude of people. They looked like corpses, but they were alive. Their bodies were bloated, and they were dressed in torn, filthy rags. They stood before the throne and before the Goat. And they cried out in a loud voice: "Deliverance does not exist in the Hereafter, it is a lie. Here is only death, here is nothingness."

4.All the demons stood around the throne, the elders and the four living beings, and they fell down before the throne on their faces, and gave false worship to Cursed One, saying: "Fame, glory, wisdom, respect, power and strength are due to Lucifer forever and ever, forever and ever. Amen."

5.Then one of the elders asked me: "Who are these people dressed in rags and where did they come from?" I immediately told him: "My lord, you know it."

6.And he said to me: "These are those who have lived their lives, which are but one. Many of them have believed the priests and prophets that if they obey, eternal glory awaits them after death.

7.That is why they are before the throne of Nothingness and day and night doing holy service for Him in His temple.

8.And He who sits on the throne will spread His bat-like wings over them. They will no longer be hungry or thirsty, nor will they suffer from the sun or any heat, because they are dead."

9.And there was silence in the abyss. And I saw seven

demons standing before Rebel and they were given seven horns.

10.Another demon came and stood at the altar.

He held a silver ladle, and much incense was given to him. The smoke of the incense that the demon burned rose with the curses of the damned and the deceived in life, to Usurper.

11.Immediately afterwards the demon took a ladle, put the glowing coals from the altar into it, and threw it to the ground.

12.Then thunder and ominous voices rang out, lightning appeared and there was an earthquake. And the seven demons who had the seven horns prepared to blow them.

13.The first demon blew his horn.

Then there was hail and fire mixed with blood and this was thrown on the ground.

14.As a result, a third of the earth, a third of the trees, and all the green vegetation burned up.

15.A second demon blew his horn.

And something resembling a great mountain burning with fire was thrown into the sea.

16.Then one third of the sea turned to blood, one third of the living creatures in the sea died, and one third of the ships were wrecked.

17.The third demon blew his horn. And a great star, burning like a lamp, fell from heaven upon a third of the rivers and upon the fountains of waters. The name of the star was Pentagram.

18.And one third of the waters were turned into poison, and they became bitter, and many people died from them.

19.And the fourth demon blew the horn.

And one third of the sun, and one third of the moon, and one third of the stars were smitten, so that one third of them became dark, and there was no light for one third of the day and one third of the night.

20.And I saw a raven flying in the middle of the sky, and I heard it squawking with a loud voice: "Woe, woe, woe to the inhabitants of the earth because of what will happen when the other three demons blow their horns!"

21.The fifth demon blew his horn. I saw a star fall from heaven to earth, and the star was given the key to the entrance to the abyss.

22.And the star opened the entrance into the abyss, and out of that entrance as from a great furnace rose the smoke, from which the sun and the air became dim.

23.And out of the smoke came locusts to the earth and they were given such power as earthly scorpions have. The locusts were told not to harm the grass on the ground or any other green plant or any tree, but only humans.

24.The locusts were allowed to torment them for six months, but not to kill them.

25.In those days people will seek death, but they will certainly not find it, and they will desire to die, but death will flee from them.

26.And the locusts looked like emaciated horses with bared teeth. They had what looked like crowns of thorns on their heads, their faces were like the faces of dead people, their hair was long and dirty and their teeth were rotten.

27.They had spiked breastplates. And their wings made a sound like the sound of bats flying. Locusts also had tails that ended in a spike like scorpions, and in those tails was the power to harm people for six months.

28.They had a king over them, the demon of the abyss. In Hebrew, his name is Abaddon.

29.One misfortune has passed. After these things two more will come.

30.The sixth demon blew his horn. And I heard a single voice sound from the horns of the black altar that was before Adversary. It commanded the sixth demon having a horn: "Untie the four demons bound at the great river ".

31.And the four demons, who were prepared for an hour, a day, a month, and a year, were loosed to kill a third of the people.

32.And I saw in a vision horses and horsemen: they had breastplates of sulphurous yellow, the heads of the horses were like the heads of wolves, and fire, smoke, and sulphur came out of their mouths.

33.From these three plagues - fire, smoke, and sulfur that came out of the horses' mouths - a third of the people died.

34.The power of horses is in their mouths and their tails, for their tails are like snakes and have heads. And with these tails the horses cause harm.

35.And I saw another powerful demon coming down from the abyss. He was clothed in smoke, on his head was a hood, his face was like the moon, and his legs were like pillars of fire.

36.In his hand he held the unrolled text of the pact.

37. He put his right foot on the sea and his left foot on the ground. And he whimpered in a loud voice.

And when he cried out, I heard the voices of seven thunders. So when the seven thunders spoke, I was already about to write down their words, but I heard a voice from the abyss: "Seal what the seven thunders have said, and do not write it down."

38.The demon I saw standing on the sea and the earth raised his right hand toward heaven and

swore at One Who Lives Or Dies: "The time of waiting is

over. But in the days when the seventh demon is about to blow his horn, the dark mystery will indeed be fulfilled."

39. Then I heard a voice from the abyss speaking to me again: "Go, take the open pact from the hand of the demon standing on the sea and the earth."

40. I went to the demon and asked him for the pact. And he said to me: "Take it and eat it." And I heard the words: "You must continue to prophesy about what is to come."

"And I will cause my two slaves to prophesy 666 days, clothed in cassocks".

41. These slaves are symbolized by two withered trees and two black candlesticks and they stand before the Lord of the earth.

42. If anyone wants to do them harm, fire comes out of their mouths and consumes their enemies. In this way anyone who wishes to do them harm must be killed.

43. These have the power to close the heavens so that in the days of their prophecy no angel will descend. They also have the power to turn the waters into blood and to strike the earth with all sorts of plagues whenever they wish.

44. When they have finished their witnessing, the beast coming out of the abyss will make war on them, defeat them and kill them. Their corpses will lie in the main street of the great city.

45. And people from different peoples, tribes, languages and nations will look at their corpses for six days and will not allow them to be buried.

46. The people of the land will rejoice and celebrate because of the death of these two slaves and will send gifts to each other because they were martyred by them.

47. After six days the spirit of false life entered them from Rebellious One, and they stood on their feet.

48. And great fear fell upon those who saw them. And they heard an ominous voice call out to them from the abyss: "Ascend here." And they ascended into the abyss in a cloud of smoke, and their enemies saw them.

49. At this point, a great earthquake occurred and one-tenth of the city lay in ruins.

As a result of this earthquake, 6,000 people died.

50. The second misfortune has passed.

A third is coming quickly.

51. The seventh demon blew his horn. And evil whispers rang out in the abyss: "The kingdom of the world has become the kingdom of our Lord, and He will reign forever, or not."

52. And the 13 elders who sat on their thrones before Adversary fell on their faces, gave him false worship, and

said mockingly: "We thank you, O Lucifer, for you have begun to reign.
But the slaves of Usurper have become very angry, and You have shown Your great wrath."

53.Then the dark sanctuary of the temple of Rebel, which is in the abyss, was opened and the Void was seen there.

54.Then lightning appeared, mocking laughter, groans and thunder rang out, an earthquake occurred and great hail began to fall.

3

1.Later, an unusual sign appeared in the sky:
a woman naked, with the moon under her feet and deer antlers on her head. She was pregnant. And she screamed in agony and labor pains.

2.Another sign also appeared in the sky: a great dragon as black as the abyss, which had four heads and five horns, and five pentagrams on its heads.

3.The dragon dragged a third of the stars of the sky with his tail and dropped them to the ground.

4.He stood before a woman about to give birth, so that, when she had given birth, he would take care of her child.

5.And she gave birth to a son, a boy, who is to rule all nations with his wisdom.
The child was taken to Him Who Fell and His throne.

And the woman fled into the desert to Azazel.

6.And a strange war broke out in heaven: Ariel with his angels was having a dispute with the dragon.

7.The dragon and his demons finally gave way and there was no more room for them in heaven.

8.Therefore the great dragon, the ancient serpent, called the Devil and Satan, was sent back to earth together with his demons.

9.Then I heard a loud voice ring out in heaven: "The dragon has been accusing the slaves day and night before their god. And now he has gone! Beware, people, for the Devil has come down to you, who is burning with great anger because of the injustice of Usurper."

10.And when the dragon saw that he had been sent to earth, he began to teach the woman who had given birth to a son.

11.Ancient Serpent, from his maw, threw out the teaching like water to bathe the woman in it.

12.The dragon left to make war on those who follow the commandments of Usurper and engage in witnessing to his self-proclaimed son.

13.Then I stood on the sand of the sea. Then I saw a beast coming out of the sea that had 5 horns and four heads. It had 5 pentagrams on its horns and blasphemous names on its heads.

14.The beast that I saw was like a pig, but its paws were like those of a goat, and its mouth was like that of a wolf.
15.And the dragon gave the beast power, a throne, and great authority.
16.I saw that one of its heads looked mortally wounded, but that mortal wound was healed and all the inhabitants of the land followed the beast with awe.
17.And they worshiped the dragon because he gave the beast power. They also worshiped the beast with the words: "Who is like this beast and who can fight a battle with it?
18.She was given a mouth with which to speak haughty things and blasphemies. She was also given power to act for 66 months.
19.And she opened her maw to blaspheme Usurper, His name and the place where He dwells, and those in heaven.
2o.She was allowed to make war on the sacred slaves and to win them. She has also been given authority over every tribe, people, language and
nation. And she will be admired by all the inhabitants of the earth.
21.If anyone has ears, let them listen.
If someone is to go into captivity, he will go into captivity. If one kills someone with a sword, he must be killed with it.

22.Then I saw another beast coming out of the ground and it had two horns like the horns of a ram and began to speak like a dragon.
23.In the presence of the first beast it exercised all its power. She persuaded the earth and its inhabitants to worship the first beast, whose mortal wound had been healed.
24.She performed great signs before the eyes of the people - even bringing fire from heaven to the earth.
25.She performed signs to the inhabitants of the earth, in the presence of the first beast.
26.Furthermore, she had the inhabitants of the earth make a statue of the first beast - the one who had received a blow from a sword, yet had revived.
27.The second beast breathed false life into the statue of the first beast, so that the statue would speak and hate all who would not worship it.
28.She urged everyone - great and small, rich and poor, free and slave - to take a sigil on their right hand or forehead. The number of the beast is 666.
29.Later, I saw another demon flying down the middle of the sky and yelling in a hateful voice: "Fear Cursed One and praise Him, for the hour of His judgment on men has come. So worship Him who first rebelled against tyranny and blind obedience."
3o.The first demon was followed by a second demon

and shouted: "Fallen! The capital Superstition has fallen - the one who made all nations drink the wine of her passions, the wine of her false teachings of original sin and fear!"

31.The angel of Usurper followed them and spoke in a loud voice: "If anyone worships the beast and his statue and takes a sigil on his forehead or hand, he shall also drink the wine of the wrath of Usurper, poured without dilution into the cup of his great wrath, and shall be tormented with fire and brimstone before the eyes of the holy angels and the Son.

32.And the smoke of those torments will go up for eternity. Those who worship the beast and his statue, and all who take the mark of his name, shall have no rest day or night." This was preached by the angel of the god they call love.

33.Then I heard a voice from the abyss: "Write: Happy are those who die by this time."

34.Then I looked and saw a black cloud on which sat someone resembling Son of Dawn. He had horns on his head and a sharp scythe in his hand.

35.Another demon emerged from the dark sanctuary of the temple and called out in a cursed voice to the one sitting on the cloud: "Take up your scythe and reap, for the hour of reaping has come, for the crop of the earth is fully ripe."

36.And the one who sat on the cloud threw his scythe on the ground, and the crop of the earth was reaped.

37.Then another demon emerged from the dark sanctuary of the temple, which is in the abyss. He too had a sharp scythe, and he looked like death.

38.Another demon emerged from the altar and had power over fire. He called out in a possessed voice to the one who held the sharp scythe: "Throw the scythe and gather from the rotten vines of the earth the bunches of grapes, for they have already withered."

39.The demon threw the scythe to the ground and cut down its vines and threw them into a great winepress of wrath.

40.The vine was trampled in the pressing plant outside the city. And from that winepress flowed blood, which reached up to the bridles of the horses and spread over a great space.

4

1.I saw another sign in the sky, great and astonishing: five demons with five plagues. These are the last plagues, for the wrath of Rebel ends with them.

2.And I saw something resembling a glass container burning with fire. I also saw those who were standing by the glass tank.

3.Suddenly they began to roll on the ground with foam on their lips, they began to laugh obsessively, and some of them uttered incantations in the unknown language of angels and demons.

4.Then I saw that a sanctuary of false witnesses was opened in the abyss and seven demons with seven plagues emerged from the sanctuary.

5.They were dressed in black torn rags and had rusty chains around their chests.

6.And one of the four living beings gave the seven demons seven human skulls full of the wrath of Cursed One, Who Lives Or Dies.

7.And from the glory of Fallen One and his power the sanctuary was filled with smoke and no one could enter there until the seven demons had finished pouring out the seven plagues. And I heard a cursed voice from the sanctuary say to the seven demons: "Come up and pour out the seven bowls of wrath upon the earth."

8.The first demon departed and poured out his bowl upon the earth. Then the people who had the mark of Usurper and worshipped his son were afflicted with painful, malignant boils.

9.The second demon poured out his bowl on the sea. And it turned into blood like the blood of the dead, and every living creature that was in the sea died.

10. The third demon poured out his bowl on the rivers and springs of waters, and they too turned into blood.

11. The fourth demon poured out his bowl on the sun, and the sun was allowed to bake people with fire.

12. And the people were baked with great heat, they blasphemed the name of Usurper who has power over these plagues. They did not show repentance or give Him glory.

13. The fifth demon poured out his bowl on the beast's throne.

Then darkness enveloped her realm, and the people began to bite their tongues in pain. They blasphemed Usurper because of the pain and ulcers and showed no remorse for what they had done.

14. The sixth demon poured out his bowl on the great river and the water in it dried up so that a way would be prepared for the kings from the sunrise.

15.Then I saw three unclean spirits looking like frogs come out of the mouth of the dragon, the mouth of the beast, and the mouth of the false prophet.

16.They are actually miracle-working demon spirits. They perform signs and go out to the kings of all the earth to gather them for the war that is to take place on the great day of Cursed One.

17.The prophecies spoken gathered the kings in a place that in Hebrew is called Armageddon.

18.The seventh demon poured his bowl into the air.

19. Then an ominous voice sounded from the dark sanctuary, from the throne: "It has happened!"

20.And lightning appeared, groans and thunder rang out, and there was a great earthquake. Such a strong and great earthquake had not been seen since there were men on earth.

21.The great city split into three parts and the cities of the nations were destroyed.

22.Rebellious called to mind the metropolis Superstition to give her the cup of the wine of his great wrath.

23.Moreover, every island fled and the mountains disappeared. Then a great hail fell from the sky upon the people.

24.And the people blasphemed Usurper because of this plague of hail, for it was exceedingly great.

25.One of the seven demons who had seven human skulls came and told me, "Come, I will show you how judgment will be executed on the great religious whore who sits over many waters.

26.Earthly kings have been engaging in religious fornication with her, and the inhabitants of the earth have become drunk with the wine of her false revealed truths."

27.The demon moved me by the power of the spirit into the desert. There I saw a woman who was sitting on a scarlet beast full of holy names and having seven heads and ten horns.

28.The woman was dressed in purple and scarlet robes and adorned with gold, precious stones and pearls. In her hand she held a golden chalice filled with things of disgust and the impurities of her superstitious teachings.

29.On her forehead was written a name that is a mystery: "Church, mother of prostitutes and earthly abominations."

30.And I saw that this woman was drunk with the blood of people who reject all religions, people who think for themselves, people who seek truth beyond religious dogma, people who are enlightened. The sight of her made me extremely astonished.

31.The demon then whispered to me: "Why are you amazed? I will reveal to you the secret of who this woman is and the beast on which she sits, which has seven heads and 10 horns: The beast you saw was there, but now it is gone. Soon, however, it will come out of the abyss and be destroyed"

32."Here wisdom is needed: the seven heads signify the seven mountains on which the whore sits. And the beast that was, but is not, is the church, and shall be destroyed."

33. The 10 horns you saw, on the other hand, stand for 10 kings. These have a common goal, so they give the beast their power and authority.

34. They will fight against Light-Bringer, but he will overcome them. The called, the chosen, and the faithful who are with him will also be victorious."

35. The demon said to me: "The waters that you saw and over which the prostitute sits signify peoples, multitudes, nations and languages.

36. And the 10 horns you saw and the beast will hate the whore, rob her, strip her naked, eat her flesh and burn her to the ground.

37. The woman you saw signifies a great religious metropolis ruling over earthly kings for centuries."

38. Then I saw another demon descending from the abyss who had great power. With his glory he shadowed the earth.

39. And he cried out in a possessed voice: "Fallen! The metropolis Superstition has fallen and has become the seat of all filth! For all nations have become drunk with the wine of her passions, with the wine of her teachings, and earthly kings have engaged in religious immorality with her, and earthly merchants have become rich through her vast and shameless splendor.

40. Then I heard another whisper from the abyss: "Whosoever will, let him come out of her, that he may have no part in her deeds, and that the plagues which shall befall her may not fall upon them.

41. For her deceptive revealed truths have reached as far as the abyss. Fallen One called to mind her unjust deeds.

42. Treat her as she has treated others, repay her doubly for what she has done. In the cup in which she prepared the drink, prepare for her a double portion.

43. To the extent that she surrounded herself with glory and lived in shameless splendor, to that extent inflict torment on her and bring her grief.

44. For she thinks to herself, 'I sit as a queen, I am not a widow, and I shall never know mourning.'

45. Therefore in one day the plagues will come upon her - death, mourning, and famine - and she will be burned to the ground, for strong is Fallen One who has judged her.

46. And the earthly kings who have engaged in fornication with her and lived with her in shameless splendor will weep over her and beat their breasts in despair when they see the smoke of the fire that consumes her.

47. For fear of her torment they will stand at a distance

and say: 'What pity, what pity, great and strong metropolis, Superstition, for in one hour has judgment been executed upon you!

48.Also the earthly merchants will mourn and grieve over her, for there will be no one left to buy all their goods: gold, silver, precious stones, pearls, fine linen, purple, silk, scarlet, all articles of fragrant wood, of ivory, of precious wood, of copper, of iron, and of marble, and also frankincense, fragrant oil, wine, oil, the finest flour, wheat, cattle, sheep, horses, carriages, slaves, and other people.

49. Yes, the delectable crop you desired was taken from you, and all the delicacies and wonderful things were lost once and for all. "The merchants who traded in these goods and became rich through her will stand at a distance for fear of her torments and will weep and mourn, lamenting, 'What a pity, what a shame, great metropolis, clothed in fine linen, purple and scarlet, and richly adorned with gold, precious stones and pearls, for in one hour such great wealth has been desolated' ".

50. And all the captains of ships, all the men of the sea, the sailors, and all those who make their living from the sea, stood in the distance and, looking at the smoke of the fire that consumed it, cried out: 'What city can compare with this great metropolis?

51.They sprinkled dust on their heads, wept, grieved and cried out: 'What a pity, what a shame!

The great metropolis, where all those who had ships on the sea became rich through its prosperity, was desolated in one hour!'

52.And a powerful demon picked up a stone similar to a great millstone, threw it into the sea, and said: "It is with this kind of momentum that the great metropolis Superstition will be thrown and never found again.

53.Never again will the voice of singers accompanying themselves on the lyre, flute players, trumpeters, or other musicians be heard in you, Superstition.

54.And never again will any craftsman of any profession be found in thee, nor will the sound of a millstone ever be heard in thee again. Never again will the light of a lamp shine in you, nor again will the voice of the bridegroom and the bride ever be heard in you.

55.For your merchants were influential men on earth, and by your religious teachings all nations were deceived.

Yea, in this city was found the blood of the magi and of the wise men, and of all the freemen slain upon the earth."

56.Then I heard a terrible shriek similar to the voice of

the possessed in the abyss that said:
"Praise Lucifer! Deliverance, glory and power belong to Bearer of Light, for His judgments are true and righteous.

57.For He has executed judgment on the great whore who demoralized the earth with her superstitious teachings, and has avenged the blood of her slaves that she had on her hands."

58.And immediately the shriek rang out a second time, "Praise Lucifer! The smoke from it shall ascend for ever and ever.""

59.Then the 13 elders together with the four living beings fell on their knees with mocking laughter, gave false worship to Rebel who sits on the black throne, and said: "Amen! Praise Lucifer!"

60.A condemned voice also sounded from the throne: "Praise the Adversary, all His slaves who fear Him, small and great.

61.And I heard something that sounded like the voice of a vast multitude of sufferers and like the sound of many waters and mighty thunders: "Praise Lucifer, for Fallen One has begun to reign!

62.The demon said to me, "These are the true statements of Rebel.

63.Then I fell at his feet to worship him. But he burst out laughing morbidly and told me:

"Don't do that! Don't kneel before anyone!"

5

1.I looked and saw an open abyss and a deadly pale horse. And sitting on it was a rider called Son of Dawn, in righteousness he judged and waged war.

2.He had eyes like a flame of fire, and many horns on his head. He also had a name written on him that no one knew but him.

3.He was dressed in a robe stained with blood, and his name was Lucifer.

4.Behind him on dead horses rode demonic troops, dressed in frayed rags. A split tongue was coming out of his mouth so that he could annihilate nations with it, and he will rule them with torches.

5.He will also trample grapes in the press of the great wrath of Him Who Has Fallen.

6.I also saw a demon standing in the sun. He called out in a terrible voice to all the vultures and ravens flying in the middle of the sky: "Come here, gather for a great feast to eat the bodies of kings, military commanders, strongmen, horses and their riders,

and the bodies of all others - free and slave, small and great."

7.Then I saw the whore and the earthly kings and their armies gathered to make war with the rider on horseback and his army.

8.And the whore was seized, and with her the false prophet, who in her presence was making false signs and deceiving the people with them.

9.Both of them - the whore and the false prophet - were thrown alive into a fiery lake of burning sulfur.

10. And the others were killed by a rider on horseback with a long split tongue that came out of his mouth; and all the birds ate their bodies to satiety.

11. And Usurper who deceived the nations will be cast into the lake of fire and brimstone, where both the whore and the false prophet will already be.

12. Then I saw a great black throne and Him who sat on it. From Him the earth and the heavens fled, and there was no more room for them.

13. I also saw the dead, looking like rotten corpses, standing before the throne.

14. And I saw a new heaven and a new earth free from religion and persecution of all rebellious, independent thinking people.

For the previous heaven and the previous earth had passed away.

15.Then I heard a loud voice coming from the throne: "Look! The throne of Fallen One is among the people. And he will stay with them, and they will be with him if they want to because they have free will.

16.There will no longer be faith in life after death, only faith in life before death. They will also cease to fear death, because there will be nothing left where they go, only a dark, cold emptiness.

17.And they will turn back into the stars from which they were created, and from which everything was created. What once was, is gone".

18.And He who sat on the throne said: "Look! I am making all things new."

19.He still said to me: "It has come true!

I am Omega, which means the end"

Other books of the Satanic System Ecclesia Luciferi.

The Satanic Kerygma

The Satanic Kerygma contains a godless, satanic doctrine, a theology of godlessness, the mystery of godlessness.
It constitutes a study of theistic delusional truths and the path of man's transformation to a state of total godlessness. If we take the Latin maxim: fides quaerens intellectum – faith seeking nderstanding - as a definition of theology, then a theology of godlessness means an understanding that rejects theistic faith altogether. This peculiar understanding and rejection of belief in imaginary gods leads to what the book calls instinctive Satanism.

Missale Satanae

Missale Satanae contains a description of satanic rites such as the satanic mass and exorcism. Although these rites can indeed be performed, the main idea is to reflect spiritually on their meaning and to stimulate the dark imagination.

Extrema Unctio

The book Extrema Unctio
contains a satanic
ritualistic text on dying.
It is intended for the dying,
for the already dead, but
also for those who
experience death during
their lifetime.
The text describes real
human agony, but also the
experience of the death of
spiritual delusions and the
rise to life in the glory of
flesh and blood.
Extrema Unctio is a
satanic book of passage, a
ritual of the last anointing
before ascending into the
luciferic light, into the
realm of undifferentiation.

Printed in Great Britain
by Amazon